SWIPE RIGHT

SWIPE RIGHT

CHOOSING YOUR FINANCIAL MATCH

Daniel A. Jack

and

Derek E. Woods

Foreword by
Tom Hegna

.

ISBN: 1544704046
ISBN-13: 9781544704043
Library of Congress Control Number: 2017905149
CreateSpace Independent Publishing Platform
North Charleston, South Carolina

CONTENTS

FOREWORD

Whatever happened to "happily ever after"? Remember all the books that you read to your children and grandchildren? They all seemed to end "and they lived happily ever after." If you think about it, retirement used to be like that. You would work for a company for thirty or forty years, and then your employers would hold a retirement party for you, present you with a shiny gold watch in front of your peers, and send you a nice check every single month for the rest of your life in the form of a pension. Wow! You could take a cruise, join the country club, and live happily ever after.

Your retirement is not going to look like that. Unless you work for the government, you are unlikely to have any significant pension. So your retirement will not depend on the success of your former employer; it will really depend on how much money you have been able to save and whether you can turn that money into enough income to last you the rest of your life. If you take out too much, you will run out of money. If you don't take out enough, you will live a "just in case" retirement.

This is what *Swipe Right: Choosing Your Financial Match* is all about. First, this book will show you how to grow and protect your money—but more importantly, *why* you need to protect it. Daniel Jack and Derek Woods will show you *how* to find the right financial advisor or coach. Most of all, they will help give you peace of mind and certainty for your future.

See, for most retirees, retirement can be a scary place. Their entire working lives, they have *saved* money and *invested* money, but they never really learned how to *distribute* money. In fact, many retirees don't really want to distribute money. They don't want to touch their principal. They want to remain in control of their money. Many times, they are simply setting themselves up for failure and will spend either too much or not enough.

With Daniel and Derek as your guides, you will have your own GPS to show you exactly where you are, where you should be going, and what the safest way is to get there. They will teach you how to find the right company and financial coach. There are so many companies and advisors out there. How can you be sure you are choosing the right ones? This book gives you the questions to ask and the boxes to check to make sure you are working with the right team.

In my public TV special, *Don't Worry, Retire Happy! Seven Steps to Retirement Security*, I talk about how important it is to have a plan. People who plan for their retirement are more confident about their retirement, they are happier in retirement, and most importantly, they are more successful in retirement than those who don't have a plan.

I also talk about how important it is to use a trusted financial professional. Retirement is not a do-it-yourself project. Hey, I'll bet you don't do your own dental work in your garage with your drill set, and I don't think you should be doing your own retirement planning, either. Retirement happens to be just as important as complicated dental work.

The retirement landscape is changing quickly; companies are adding new products, benefits, and features every day. How can you keep up with all of this? You can't. You need a professional who does this every day. Look, I am considered a retirement-income expert by many, and I use a financial professional. Why? Because even though I know what I need to do to retire optimally, I don't follow the day-to-day changes in product offerings. Besides, retirement is so important that I want a second set of eyes on my plan. I get busy, and I need someone to remind me that it is time to review the plan as well. You should do the same.

So, what are some of the risks? The riskiest time to invest in the market is right before or right after your retirement. If the stock market crashes then, would that affect your retirement plan? Inflation could decimate the purchasing power of the income that you have been able to generate with your savings. Can you live on half your income? That is what 4 percent inflation does to purchasing power over a twenty-year period.

Some people think that because the market has averaged over 10 percent per year since 1926, they can withdraw 10 percent, or 8 percent, or 6 percent—well, surely 4 percent per year, right? Nope. Those numbers will likely have you running out of money before you run out of breath. Morningstar says the safe withdrawal rate is 2.8 percent per year.

What about the need for long-term care? Long-term-care services are very expensive. What happens if you need some care? Is that in your plan? There is a 72 percent chance you will need care. And what about the granddaddy of all retirement risks—longevity? What would happen to your plan if medical technology continues to develop cures and solutions for our medical problems? What if you live to age 100 or 110? Those Monte Carlo simulations your broker put together assumed age ninety. Almost 100 percent of them will fail if you live to age ninety-five or one hundred.

Make no mistake—millions, no, tens of millions of people will be ambushed by one or more of these risks. But not you! What Daniel and Derek do in this book is share not only the risks that are out there, but also some very simple solutions—ways that you can take these risks off the table.

I give public seminars all across the country. I, too, am on a mission to help people avoid these risks. Many people think retirement is so complicated. I disagree. In fact, I believe the ultimate success of your retirement will depend on your answers to two simple questions:

1.   How much guaranteed lifetime income do you have?
2.   Have you taken the key retirement risks off the table?

See, the success of your retirement is not about your assets. This is a paradigm shift. For years, you were taught that the bigger your pile of money, the better your retirement would be. That is not necessarily true. Your assets can be lost, stolen, swindled out of you, taken in a lawsuit or divorce, or decimated in a market crash. The ultimate success of your retirement will really depend on how much income you have and if you have properly protected yourself from the many risks in retirement. Daniel and Derek help you do just that.

By using the financial solutions Daniel and Derek discuss, you can set up an optimal plan—one where you are thoroughly protected and will never run out of money. One where you have financial peace of mind. One where you know that you have minimized or eliminated key risks. And one where you leave the right amount of money to the right people when you die.

I have been training financial advisors for over thirty years and speaking about retirement to clients all around the world. I've written four books on retirement. All of my books have the same common theme: your retirement does not need to be complicated. Proper retirement planning can be based on math and science.

If you are looking for an enlightened perspective on retirement beyond the traditional sense, put aside some time immediately to read this future best seller. Once you understand how simple retirement is, you will have plenty of time to enjoy it with your grandchildren instead of sweating every time you open the business section of the paper.

On a personal note, I have known Daniel and Derek for over fifteen years. They are considered top-shelf professionals by their peers. I love the fun way they present their material. Please enjoy this book, and then hand it to a friend. Put their ideas to work, and you will have a happy and successful retirement!

February 2017
Tom Hegna
Author and economist
www.tomhegna.com

PREFACE

Throughout this book, you'll see the term *financial coach* frequently used. In the financial-services industry, financial professionals go by numerous titles. You'll come across insurance agents, financial advisors, mortgage consultants, investment planners, investment advisors, and stockbrokers, just to name a few. These terms have generally accepted and sometimes specific legal definitions associated with them.

The term *financial coach* is less tangible. It is not a legal definition we are striving for here. Rather, it is a mind-set. An excellent coach will help you live the best financial life you can live. And he will always put your needs as a client ahead of his needs as a coach. Any of the financial professionals just listed could meet the criteria of a good coach. You just have to find the right one. This book will help you.

INTRODUCTION

D ating websites and smartphone apps have become very popular during the past decade. Several of the more popular sites have successfully added the terms *swipe right* and *swipe left* to the English vernacular. Whether you are in your twenties or your sixties, these sites make it easy to look at pictures and read quick biographies.

Collectively, this information allows you to efficiently decide if the man or woman you are looking at might have similar hobbies, interests, faith, education, or attractiveness, or if he or she just looks like fun. If you don't like what you see, then swipe left as fast as possible. But if someone has piqued your interest, then swipe right and hope you receive the same response. The whole idea is to find your match!

When it comes to money, finances, financial plans, and financial advisors, many people tend to swipe right when they should be swiping left, and other times they don't swipe at all and just give up. Humans tend to be attracted to certain things for the wrong reasons. We let emotions and shiny objects drive our decision-making, rather than a process with a well-thought-out, rational plan. Welcome to being a normal person.

When we started talking about this book, it revolved around one central idea: how do we help people manage the emotional side of financial decision-making? We want to make sure you are swiping right when the right plan and right financial coach match you and your goals.

With your financial-planning goals, there is little room for error. The older you get and the closer to a particular goal you become, the more important good decision-making becomes. For some financial goals like retirement, you only get one shot. Just one. You have to get it right. Your future self, your dignity, your health, your happiness, and your family legacy all depend on getting it right.

How you save and how you invest are only a part of it. The most significant piece of getting it right is understanding your financial temperament. More than you know, how you react and make financial decisions during chaotic markets or life events significantly impacts your probability of success.

There are several ways people can save, invest, and protect themselves. Hopefully, these include putting money aside and paying off debt. There are also quite a few ways a retiree can convert assets into income during retirement. The best way to approach any of these activities, though, is going to be a balanced strategy that doesn't create any unnecessary emotional or financial stress.

While you are working, you want to make sure you are setting enough aside in the proper places while still being able to enjoy life. When it comes to taking out money in your later years, you don't want to withdraw so much that you go broke, or take out so little that you fail to attain the retirement success you've worked so hard to earn.

Choosing the right strategy means knowing yourself. This can be harder than you realize. Every one of us makes decisions that are influenced by our past experiences, upbringings, values, and beliefs. The complicated psychological term for this is called *bias*. Many times, we are unaware of how those things cause us to make certain choices.

You can end up designing a plan without taking your personality fully into account. A plan might look good on paper, but if it isn't a match for your temperament, then it will fail. This book is designed to help you match the right strategy for how *you* think.

UCLA's legendary former basketball coach John Wooden defined success the following way: "Success is the peace of mind that is a direct result of self-satisfaction in knowing you made the effort to become the best you are capable of becoming." We want as many people as possible to be financial successes. That will only occur if you make the effort to be your best financial self.

As it relates to your financial life, that means you need to take the time to equip yourself with the essential information to be a success. No more and no less. Due to the sheer volume of information and the time required to sift through it all, you need to find a competent financial coach to guide you on your financial journey.

Most of us never took a class in high school or college on how to handle our finances or find a financial advisor. We ask our friends or consult the Internet for advice, and even with all of that information, we still have a level of uncertainty as to whether we have the best plan.

You should be able to control the things you can and be at peace with the things you can't. Control is a big deal, a really big deal. It is hard to feel relaxed, reassured, and at peace when you feel like there's so much uncertainty. Making sure you stay in as much control of your future as possible, as well as helping you find peace of mind about your financial plan, is one of our goals.

When you are twenty-five years old and you make a mistake financially, then you've got about forty years to absorb the negatives before conquering retirement. But when you make a mistake near or in retirement, the financial clock may be close to striking midnight, meaning you have to live with the consequences. No one plans to live solely off Social Security in their golden years, yet many do. The decisions they made years ago helped create their unenviable situations.

If you have not prepared properly, a consequence might be reentering the workforce when you're in your seventies or selling your home and moving into a much more meager residence. It could mean losing vital access to quality medical care, as well as losing the means to spend time the way you choose. Why do some people drastically change their standards of living when they get to retirement? The answer is that they have to.

How do you make sure you aren't one of those that have to? One of the best ways is to make sure you have a financial coach. If you are partnered with a well-educated and experienced financial planner, you are much more likely to avoid making big financial mistakes.

Like any good fitness coach, a talented professional will help you make decisions today that contribute to your long-term success. He or she accomplishes this by knowing not just what the best options are, but who you are as a person and how your choices fit your behaviors. So, take control of your personal finances, and find a great financial coach.

The other way to help secure your future is to put your money where it receives the best leverage. Knowing which of your planning options provides the greatest efficiency and emotional reassurance for your situation has as much of an impact as having the right coach. You need to make the right decision on both.

We have been seated on every side of the financial-services table. We've purchased financial products as consumers, and we have implemented solutions as financial coaches. We've worked in management from the insurance and investment-company perspective, and one of us has worked as a chief securities regulator to ensure transparency and suitability for the consumer. This book is our nearly forty years of combined experience in financial services to help guide you toward the best decisions for you and your family.

There are more than enough personal-finance books already available loaded with great information. However, they usually are simply too long, or they are marred by biases in favor of the types of financial practices or products that their particular authors advocate. We have endeavored to provide guidance when there are nuanced gray areas in the planning process.

More importantly, whenever possible, we've confidently shared our very firm convictions when a particular strategy or financial product provides only a black or white solution. This book ultimately ensures you have enough of the right information to make educated decisions, so you know when to swipe right or swipe left!

CHAPTER 1
PLAN IT

Before beginning, plan carefully.
—CICERO, ROMAN ORATOR AND POLITICIAN, FIRST CENTURY BC

*A man who does not think and plan long
ahead will find trouble right at his door.*
—CONFUCIUS, CHINESE PHILOSOPHER, FIFTH CENTURY BC

A goal without a plan is just a wish.
—ANTOINE DE SAINT-EXUPÉRY, FRENCH
WRITER, TWENTIETH CENTURY

This next comment will sound extremely basic. But we want to get it out of the way early. *You will simply do better if you have a plan.* More specifically, this should be a written plan that reflects your goals and risk tolerance. It is remarkable how this essential fact is completely lost on people as it pertains to their finances.

Is there a truly meaningful task that you have accomplished in the past where, in hindsight, you wish you would have just flown by the seat of your pants? Of course not. We bet no one reading this book right now, when thinking about something essential to your life, career, family, or faith, can honestly say, "Geez, I wish I would have winged it instead of thinking ahead of time and planning what I wanted to say!"

Consider for a moment all the things for which you plan. We won't make you raise your hand in front of everyone, but if you were being administered various enhanced interrogation techniques, you know you would unhappily admit that you have spent more time planning your family vacations than you have spent planning your potentially thirty-year-long retirement. Taking it even further, you might have even binge-watched shows on Netflix like *House of Cards* or *Breaking Bad* for more hours than you spent retirement planning.

When you take a summer vacation to a Disney resort, a hike in the mountains, or even a trip to the lake, do you plan beforehand how you'll travel there, or do you just show up at the airport and buy tickets, or hop in the car and take off to your destination one day? Do you pack a suitcase and check the weather report? We think you probably do plan at least a little bit.

If your child or grandchild is having a birthday party, do you send out invitations and then go a few days early and buy party hats, gifts, and an ice-cream cake, perhaps? We think you do. How about the grocery store? Do you write down a grocery list before you go? We think you usually do. Back in high school, did you go get your prom dress or tuxedo bought or reserved early? We think you went early.

And surely you have planned or will plan a wedding. Well, for clarification, we are assuming this alleged union didn't happen in Las Vegas. If it did, we fully acknowledge you may not have had a plan. What about your kids? When your children were born, did you put the crib together, set up the changing table, and decorate the baby's room before or after your child's birth? We think it was a few months before.

Here's another way to think about it: if you don't have written goals, then how will you know when you've successfully arrived? You don't wing it when it matters. You can't, and you know you can't. Instead, you "Plan It" when it matters. Your finances and retirement matter, a lot actually. If the light bulb just went off in your head, and you realized that your money world needs some additional forethought, then we don't need to beat a dead horse. We all now accept that we need to "Plan It," so let's get started.

The Planning Premium
The parameters of a solid and effective financial plan are laid out by ONE Retirement's CEO, Ron Sanders, AIF®. Ron says, "If you want to be

financially independent, you have to start with a plan. A great financial plan has both the flexibility that allows you to adapt to changes in your life, and the discipline to keep you on track during turbulent times."

The value of this planning is illustrated quite well by using retirement weekends as an example. Take a quick moment and think about what you are planning to do this coming weekend. (That's right, *gotcha*—you often even plan your weekends in advance!) As you look out toward those weekends in retirement, you must understand that "starting a financial plan is possibly the most critical decision" of your financial life. "Those [people] with a financial plan in place and seek[ing] professional advice are the best off financially," with significantly more in retirement assets than the average.[1]

HSBC Bank is a well-respected, New York–based corporate bank. They published an exhaustive study in 2011 that surveyed 17,849 financial trendsetters across seventeen developed countries. The survey was very insightful when it comes to retirement planning habits.[2]

Most importantly, HSBC discovered that the value of retirement savings is significantly higher for those who have a financial plan and seek advice versus those who don't. This extra retirement savings is what HSBC now calls the Planning Premium.[3] Basically, if you want a whopping 69 percent higher Planning Premium, then you shouldn't wing it.

As retirement expert Tom Hegna discusses in one of his broadcasts, *Don't Worry, Retire Happy! Seven Steps to Retirement Security*, it is actually steady income in retirement that makes people happy.[4] Specifically, 73 percent of HSBC respondents agree with Tom by saying that not having to worry about money is the single biggest key to achieving a happy retirement.[5]

It is not just a huge 69 percent increase in retirement savings that represents the Planning Premium benefit; there are further benefits as well. Investors with financial plans have nearly six times more total retirement assets or 552 percent more than Non-Planners.[6] Yes, you read that correctly. We said 552 percent more. If you could get a 552 percent raise at work, you would take it in a second!

Again, the Planning Premium is having more income, savings, and assets, which are all quantified as hard benefits. These hard benefits occur when you have a financial plan. However, the Planning Premium includes additional soft benefits that reflect a more positive outlook and fewer worries about retirement. It isn't just a few nonmonetary benefits, though.

Soft benefits associated with the Planning Premium have remarkable breadth. US citizens surveyed who own a financial plan report greater freedom, happiness, opportunity, hope, wealth, and health, while at the same time reporting less fear, loneliness, and financial hardship.[7] Ultimately, the people who plan have more of the good stuff and less of the bad stuff.

Soft Benefits of Planning

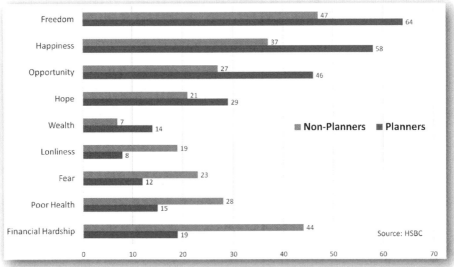

Source: HSBC

Among the information discovered, 50 percent of people do not have a financial plan, and the biggest reason given was because people didn't think they had enough money. Additionally, 54 percent of men but only 44 percent of women have a financial plan.[8]

The survey found that people could be categorized into one of four different consumer types. The first group is made up of 38 percent of the respondents, and they are called "Non-Planners: Disengaged."[9] They are just like they sound. They don't have a professionally created financial plan and put little to no time into retirement planning on their own. Think of the guy who shows up late to the party without a gift every time. And worse yet, he doesn't even realize it's a problem!

The second group represents 12 percent of people, and they are labeled "Non-Planners: Advice Seekers."[10] This group also does not have a financial plan, and while they do not seek out holistic advice, they do look for professional financial advice regarding a particular need from time to time. Ladies, this is your dear girlfriend who always asks for dating advice on guys, but who never actually follows your instructions.

Another 22 percent of people make up the third group, which is named "Planners: Active Self-Guided."[11] This group is Internet savvy and has a financial plan but does not seek further professional advice. These are like the self-diagnosing WebMD people. By the end of their self-evaluation, they either need to take two aspirin or rush to the ER for an appendectomy. They have no real idea if their plan is right or not.

The final 28 percent of people fall into the category listed as "Planners: Advice-Seekers." These folks have a financial plan and seek professional financial advice. They are well prepared for retirement and are more likely to be older and wealthier.[12] Apparently, with age does come some additional wisdom. These people are like the contestants on the popular television show *Shark Tank* who don't quibble over giving up another 5 percent stake in their business. They are smart enough to know getting the additional 552 percent in Planning Premium is worth the partnership.

Optimism abounds for people that are planners. The survey found that 53 percent of them viewed retirement as a time of freedom, compared with much lower percentages for Non-Planners. In fact, Non-Planners perceive retirement as a time of financial hardship.[13] Finally, Non-Planners are nearly twice as likely to be very worried that they will not be able to cope financially in retirement.[14]

The Four Consumer Types

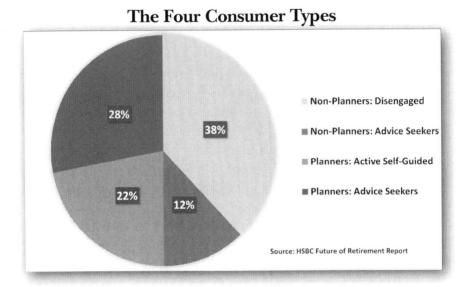

28%

38%

22%

12%

Non-Planners: Disengaged

Non-Planners: Advice Seekers

Planners: Active Self-Guided

Planners: Advice Seekers

Source: HSBC Future of Retirement Report

Earlier in this chapter, we discussed how important having a semblance of control is to living a happy and fulfilling retirement. Unfortunately, "the message which is being lost on Non-Planners is that for many of them, it is within their power to take the necessary steps to ensure that they avoid financial hardship."[15]

Likewise, the study showed that across the board, Planners: Advice Seekers have higher participation rates in defined benefit plans, defined contribution plans, individual personal pensions, mutual funds and investments, insurance, cash savings accounts, bonds, and employee stock plans.[16] All of these add up to create that Planning Premium we all should want.

So Why the Hesitation?

Taking control requires a plan and appropriate goal setting. Stephanie R. Summers, RFC, MBA, is a financial advisor at Kramer Wealth Managers based in Frederick, Maryland. In her publication entitled *Financial Planning Basics*, she uses the acronym SMART to describe that for a financial plan to work, it must be *S*pecific, *M*easurable, *A*ttainable, *R*elevant, and *T*imely.[17] Ms. Kramer's SMART acronym fits well with the Practical Behavioral Model discussed in HSBC's survey findings. This model demonstrates a very basic rule that whatever people are being asked to do must be considered realistic and achievable.[18]

Financial Planning Basics

- **<u>S</u>pecific**
- **<u>M</u>easurable**
- **<u>A</u>ttainable**
- **<u>R</u>elevant**
- **<u>T</u>imely**

Source: Stephanie R. Summers, RFC, MBA
Kramer Wealth Managers

We think that too often advisors use cookie-cutter planning models or fall into old habits instead of getting to know the clients to know what will be most effective for them. Here is the dilemma: without truly knowing a client, it is impossible for an advisor to set attainable goals. And without knowing all the elements that need to go into a proper financial plan, it is impossible for a person to set up a plan by him or herself.

We will talk more about the necessity of a good partnership between a client and financial coach later in the book. But here in the next few paragraphs, we will share some of the reasons people hesitate to embrace a written financial plan.

Pitfalls

OK, when it comes to pitfalls, here comes an unpleasant poke in the chest. Take a deep breath. Are you ready? The biggest pitfall is *you*. Sorry. Don't take it personally. It isn't that you aren't smart enough. You're plenty smart. It is that all of us have emotional responses to events that impact our decision-making. And because money, like your children and health, is intensely personal, your emotions play a greatly enhanced role.

You will exacerbate your pitfalls if your plan on paper doesn't match your temperament. By temperament we mean, are you a paralysis-by-analysis person? Do you see a six-hundred-point drop in the market and get scared, or do you simply think, "It's only a 3 percent drop, and I don't need income now anyway, so who cares?" Do you live in denial, thinking you aren't going to become disabled or die? These are all ugly, snaring pitfalls that you must address. If you don't, then the scientific term is that *you're screwed!*

Here are a few more pitfalls. Data clearly shows that procrastination can derail the planning process. Delaying important decisions can often be a greater threat to a married household than for single people.

Usually the reason is that married people either can't agree or they end up talking each other out of a good idea. Households with two people involved in the joint decision-making process are more likely to postpone getting financial advice than households with a sole decision-maker.[19]

It is therefore critical that "where financial decision-making is shared it needs to be clear who is responsible for implementing each part of the plan."[20] Along those lines, accountability is critical to a financial plan. Lack of accountability is going to prevent a plan from being created, and it will kill a plan if it already exists.

Low literacy rates regarding personal finance is a common pitfall that can contribute to misperceptions about financial planning. These abysmal literacy rates can lead to a misunderstanding of costs. "Consumers often overestimate the cost of likely insurance premiums by up to three times compared to what they actually will be expected to pay."[21]

Understandably, many people think the planning process is too overwhelming. It's difficult to start a plan when you don't even know where to begin. Other people shy away because they don't want to create a failure in their lives. Starting a plan but not finishing it doesn't feel very good.

Remember, though, you don't have to have a 100 percent success rate on every planning objective. Creating a plan, implementing it, and only hitting 70 percent of your goals is still progress. An important aspect of staying on task is to keep the plan simple, flexible, and yours. And don't forget that the plan must be achievable.

Immediate gratification plays into retirement planning in a negative way as well. For an example of immediate gratification, just look back to our Netflix binge-watching observation. Getting what we want when we want it is part of our electronically dependent and overly connected culture. Texts are a great display of this sense of immediacy; 90 percent of all texts are read within five minutes.[22]

Relating this culture trait to finances means it is very challenging for people today to see planning and saving for what they really represent. Planning and saving don't mean saying no. They mean saying yes to your future self. Foregoing instant gratification now by planning and saving today and therefore spending less means fewer worries and reduced stress tomorrow.

It also means more freedom and, most importantly, more spending later. We aren't smart enough to come up with the next physics proof, like $E = MC^2$ or $F = MA$. However, we have done this long enough to know that *Saving Now = Spending More Later!*

Summary
You have now read about the inarguable soft and hard benefits of owning a financial plan. You also know why some people fail to plan. Because of your interest in learning more about retirement decision-making, we are pretty sure that no matter where you sit financially, as you're reading this book, you don't want to have less of a lifestyle on your retirement date than you have right now. You want to have more money, perhaps much more. That means that whatever you've got needs to grow between now and then. It is time to swipe right on having a financial plan, because our next objective is to "Grow It."

CHAPTER 2

GROW IT

Money, like emotions, is something you must
control to keep your life on the right track.
—NATASHA MUNSON, CEO OF BE MAGIC INC.

I can calculate the motion of heavenly bodies
but not the madness of people.
—SIR ISAAC NEWTON, SEVENTEENTH CENTURY PHYSICIST

Because there is so much out there on investing, we have decided to strip this topic down to the mere essentials. But whether you're a do-it-yourself investor or a seasoned financial advisor, here's the catch: the essentials of investing aren't what you think.

Investing is the financial topic that is probably more often written about than all the other topics in this book combined. Rightfully so, because whether you are entering your twenties or approaching ninety, you need to learn about investing. There are plenty of quality, factual treatises on how to invest. Several juggernauts include *Stocks for the Long Run* by Jeremy Siegel and *The Intelligent Investor* by Benjamin Graham. Your head will hurt when you finish reading these masterpieces, but you will be so much smarter for having taken the time to do so.

If you want a great fiction book about investing, then we suggest *The Roaring 2000s* by Harry S. Dent Jr. We are kidding! That was a joke. Don't sue us. *The Roaring 2000s* isn't a fiction book. It's simply a nonfiction book that couldn't have been more wrong if it had been penned by a medieval scholar writing that the world is flat.

Anyway, if there is so much good stuff written about how to invest, then why do people often fail so miserably as investors? The answer will shock you. The most prevailing reason advisors fail their clients and clients fail themselves is because all they do is focus on the facts.

Advisors can be like Detective Sergeant Joe Friday from that old television show *Dragnet* asking for "just the facts, ma'am." We know it sounds downright weird to suggest that there's too much focus on the facts, especially when in most other areas of life, we don't see enough facts—or, worse yet, we see people making up their own facts to fit a particular narrative in sports, business, politics, or religion. Give us a moment to explain.

You've all heard of Sir Isaac Newton. He was an English mathematician, astronomer, and physicist who lived from 1643 to 1727. Among his many contributions to science were his three laws of motion. He also discovered gravity, which was no small feat, mind you, but for our purposes we're are going to focus on Newton's Third Law of Motion. It states that *for every action, there is an equal and opposite reaction.* If you've ever stepped off a boat onto a dock and noticed the boat moving away from you as you push off, then you've experienced Newton's Third Law of Motion.

Traditional books on investing, including the aforementioned ones, focus on stocks and portfolios like they are science. The conventional wisdom says that historically stocks or real estate do better than bonds, while bonds do better than fixed annuities and bank CDs. Therefore, we can look at the proven science and know that investing in stocks is the best way to make money and outpace inflation.

If we apply Newton's Third Law of Motion, then the *action* is that multiple investors sell their mutual funds, and *the equal and opposite reaction* is that the market should begin dropping accordingly because of lowered demand. That makes sense, right? Supply-and-demand theory in economics tells us that if there is less demand for something, then supply will increase, and the price will adjust and go down.

Though supply and demand theory makes perfect sense and investing facts are useful, that misses the point entirely. Granted, we are not idiots; we do agree that there's a best and most efficient way to invest.

Yes, we have heard of modern portfolio theory. Understanding stock fundamentals is critical to building a solid investment portfolio.

But that information is worthless—that's right, worthless—if the actual investor gets emotional and behaves in a way that causes his or her portfolio to cease mirroring historical stock-market growth trends. Once this mess occurs, investors' experience will feel like the stock market only goes down after they buy and up after they sell.

So, you can see that if we were to try and apply the laws of science to stock-market behavior compared to actual investor behavior, we'd have the unfortunate "Swipe Left Law of Investing," which would be something tantamount to this: "For every action, there is an equal and opposite reaction; or maybe not."

As we just informed you, many times the stock market goes up, but the investor's account doesn't go up with it because the investor bailed out of the market at the wrong time. Chalk that one up to fear. In the ensuing pages, we are going to give you lots of investing facts. These investing truths have guided millions of successful investors for several generations.

But here's what we know that almost all advisors and do-it-yourselfers miss: The truth is that the focus should not be on stock-market facts. Instead, when designing a portfolio, the whole focus should be how you emotionally respond to those stock-market facts. We'll call that the "Swipe Right Law of Investing."

In other words, when you see your 401(k) or IRA accounts that used to have $250,000 drop 20 percent, and now you only have $200,000 in them, what do you do? Very personally, what do you do? Here's what this looks like in real life. An average advisor gets out multiple colorful glossy charts illustrating stock-market performance history and says, "Don't worry. See that big drop in 2008? It was only temporary!"

However, a talented financial coach would be asking you if you would sell, get out of the water, and sit on the beach until the lifeguard says the perceived sharks are gone. Or would you remain invested, keep swimming, and continue investing more with each paycheck? The serious financial professional knows that there really aren't any sharks in the water, and his or her job is to make sure you keep swimming.

We can also show you chart after chart of stock-market history (and we're about to do so) with all the gains, corrections, losses, rebounds, and new highs. Those are historical facts. The information is necessary and can provide insightful investing ideas. They are even compliance approved, and that's really saying something. But who cares?

In your gut, you are worried and asking, "What if this time is different, and my account doesn't come back up? Or worse yet, what if it just keeps going down?" That is the thing, really. When we see big drops in our account values, it can be downright frightening, especially if we are close to needing to take out that money.

Ever since the no-load mutual fund revolution in the early 1990s, the focus has increasingly been on who has the lowest fees instead of where it should be—on investor behavior. So as a Washburn law school property professor used to say, "Let's talk turkey" about investor behavior.

Stumbling Blocks

Our goal here is to help you understand that the enemy to your financial success in the years ahead is not inflation, stock market volatility, low interest rates, or taxes. There are plenty of powerful planning mechanisms that your financial coach knows about in order to deal with those challenges. Instead, the enemy is you.

As Benjamin Graham points out, "The investor's chief problem—and even his worst enemy—is likely to be himself."[1] We agree with Mr. Graham, but more specifically, he is talking about your emotions. It is your emotions that are going to try to get you to make poor financial decisions repeatedly in the years to come.

How successful of an investor you become is going to heavily depend on your behavior. Your financial coach can put together a solid plan for you. Only you can control whether you follow your plan. The good news is that it is your money, and you can do whatever you want with your money. The bad news is that it is your money, and you are solely responsible, so you'd better make good decisions regarding your plan.

Charles D. Ellis wrote a book in 2002 titled *Winning the Loser's Game: Timeless Strategies for Successful Investing*. Mr. Ellis makes an interesting point by comparing investing to the game of tennis. He says that in professional tennis, points are won. In other words, they are earned by skillful players hitting great shots. However, in amateur tennis, points are lost. This means that most of the time, an amateur tennis player hits the ball into the net or out of bounds. Then the opponent gets a point, not because he earned it, but because the other player made a mistake. The winner will be the amateur player who makes the fewest mistakes. Mr. Ellis says investing works the same way. The investor making the fewest mistakes will win when it comes to meeting financial goals.[2]

This is where good financial coaches come into play. The advantage they bring to the table is in helping you make fewer mistakes with your money. We know one advisor who has a client that calls every time the quarterly performance report shows negative returns, just to be coached to invest more when the account value is down rather than run for the hills. It is easy to see that we should invest when the markets dips, but the facts reveal that most investors bail out instead of doubling down.

In our travels around the United States, we have discovered that people from all different backgrounds and socioeconomic statuses have minimally one thing in common: They almost all, at one point or another during their lives, have made at least one huge financial mistake they wish they could take back. They want a do-over.

In client meetings, when we ask husbands why they aren't as well-off financially as they should be, we hear things like, "I cashed out my 401(k)," or "I bought a boat we didn't need," or "We bought more house than we could afford at the wrong time," or "When the kids moved out, I remodeled one of their old rooms and filled it with expensive exercise equipment I never use." Often in those same meetings, when we ask wives why they aren't as well-off financially as they should be, we stoically hear something like, "Well, I married an idiot."

That story obviously isn't true—well, not always. It does do a good job of illustrating some of the poor decisions people make every single day when it comes to their personal finances. What is true, though, is that it takes some bravery, wisdom, and good financial guidance to accumulate wealth. There is no shortcut or silver bullet. An experienced financial coach will be able to help you maintain your bravery while adding to your wisdom.

Most of us have or have had mortgages, car payments, student loans, kids' college tuitions, doctor bills, clothes, vacations, sick parents—and the expense list goes on and on. That is called life. Accumulating wealth is difficult because you have to make good investment decisions (wisdom) and then have the discipline (bravery) to stick with those decisions. This is significant because letting fear get the best of you is what will prevent you from consistently making disciplined investing decisions. So, you gotta be brave. Bravery keeps you disciplined.

What happens more often than not is that people do the wrong thing at the wrong moment with the wrong rationale. Brad Barber and Terrance Odean wrote a compelling scholarly article called "Trading is Hazardous to Your Wealth." They researched 66,465 households from 1991 to 1996 and found that individual investors were underperforming the market. They then sought out reasons for this underperformance. They identified overconfidence, regret avoidance, and too much attention paid to one's portfolio as significant contributors to underperformance.[3]

When it comes to overconfidence, physicians provide a great example. Most doctor groups we've interacted with have implemented some type of retirement plan in their practices where they are able to self-direct their investments. It usually doesn't work because their self-directed investments rarely meet their expectations.

Overconfidence is the reason. Being able to do a quadruple-bypass surgery, deliver a premature infant, or surgically remove a brain tumor definitely places a person in an elite professional group. It's hard to even describe that type of brilliance and attention to detail. However, and this is the critical issue, the skills that make a person a brilliant surgeon have nothing to do with those making a person a wise and disciplined investor.

Another blind spot for investors is what is called reference points. Shlomo Benartzi, a professor at UCLA and chief economist at the Allianz Global Investors' Center of Behavioral Finance, says people are "exquisitely sensitive" to a reference point.[1] Dan Ariely, a professor of psychology and behavioral economics at Duke University, has established that investors can fall prey to a similar issue called the "anchoring effect."

Anchoring is a phenomenon where investors let random numbers irrationally impact their decisions. Mr. Ariely took basic office items like a stapler, notepad, and pen, and then he had students bid on each item eBay style. But before he did, he placed the last two digits of each student's Social Security number next to the items on their individual screens. Amazingly, the students with the higher last two digits in their Social Security numbers went on to bid more for each item than students with lower Social Security numbers.[5] This is due to the students subconsciously anchoring to a number they see that has no correlation to the object's actual monetary value. We agree that's weird, yet that is how the human mind works.

Like it is for a gambler, the reference point is the initial stake or anchor. With an investor, it could be his or her highest account balance or the level of the S&P 500 on the day he or she invested a large sum of money. When you hold on to that starting value, it makes you believe that you can't change anything until you get back to or above your initial stake.

That means you end up basing your decisions on an irrelevant fact. As we will discuss, different investments behave in different ways at different times. If you are anchored to a specific investment, you need to make sure there is a rationale other than that this investment is what you have bought, so it has to get back up to what you started with.

When it comes to investing, there are many other major biases contributing to poor performance, including recency, survivorship, affinity, herd mentality, hindsight, and loss aversion. Recency bias is when your mind places a premium on what happened in the market most recently. The fact is that something happening in the near past is not evidence that the same thing will happen again in the near future. Just because the market has been climbing recently does not mean it will keep climbing.

Here is a perfect example: Many times when discussing where to invest money, people will look to how a particular investment has been performing. If it has been making money, they want to put their money there. Why? Because it is making money, and that is a positive. The problem is that no one goes to the store to find what items have the highest prices; they want to buy what is on sale.

With investments, investors take that common sense and toss it out the window to make sure they own the winners, not the losers. Interestingly enough, last year's losers end up being this year's winners.

If you have fallen prey to this, don't feel bad; there is a financial publication that feeds this mentality by telling you all the big winners from the previous year. We wish they could tell us all the big winners, and get it right, for the next year.

Another bias, of which we are unusually unaware, is the affinity trap. This occurs when you place too heavy of an emphasis on trusted or well-liked individuals in your social circle. Just because your pastor, best friend at work, or close family friend thinks something is a great investment, that doesn't make it true. Our advice is that it is fine to listen to your buddies when it comes to fantasy-football picks, but it's definitely not when it comes to financial decisions.

Of all the challenges, the most common one is the need to feel like you are part of a group, and that is called herd mentality. Everyone wants friends, and there are actual pain centers in the human brain that trigger when you're alone too much. The issue is that this may cause you to make decisions because you don't want to miss out on something that others are doing. Instead, you should be making decisions based on what makes the most sense for your personality, risk tolerance, situation, and time horizon.

There is the old saying that hindsight is twenty-twenty. That is true. But hindsight bias is different—it's when you think you can use past market declines to predict exactly what the market will do in the future. This is one of the biggest contributors to the fool's errand of market timing.

Backed up by countless charts, market timers think that because they know what happened in past real-estate or technology bubbles, they can now anticipate big market changes during the next bubble. If only it were that easy. The markets may have trends, but the hardest one to predict is when you will have a loss.

Many people suffer from loss aversion. This was discovered through research back in 1979. It showed that retirees feel roughly ten times worse about losing $100 than they feel good about gaining $100. In other words, the research showed a retiree would not accept a gamble with a 50 percent chance of winning $100 and a 50 percent chance of losing $10.

The population as a whole is not this intensely risk averse. However, retired people statistically become much more risk averse in this manner.[6]

The pain from a loss feels far worse than the pleasure from a win. This mentality can result in being invested too conservatively, causing you to either miss out on necessary returns or needing to significantly increase your savings rate to compensate for the reduced growth potential.

How is that for an extensive list of emotional and mental pitfalls? If you feel like it is a daunting task to manage all these issues, then your thinking is heading down the right track. Even if you were aware of all the behaviors we listed above, which most people aren't, then you have the secondary task of staying disciplined. Good luck with that. We know professionals in our business who can't even do it after decades of knowledge and experience.

Beyond emotional challenges, another area that a financial coach can help you behave well is with mental accounting. This is when your mind compartmentalizes sources of money. You might not want to spend money locked safely away in savings, but you may not have any trouble spending cash from a new inheritance or work bonus.

By segmenting your money, you can better make it through volatile markets. If you know the market swings are only affecting your long-term buckets of money that you won't need for ten to twenty years, then you'll be better able to withstand volatility. When you forget, that is a great time to call your financial coach and review the purposes of your different buckets.

The key to your successful navigation of investing comes down to two things: a coach to guide proper behavior and as much automation as possible. If you have ever had a retirement plan that takes money out of each paycheck, you have experienced automation. When it comes to remembering or being willing to do something, people have a funny habit of forgetting or not wanting to do it.

If you set things on autopilot, you end up with much better results. This is due to the obvious fact that you do not have to make a decision each time, but you also quickly learn that making that investment is not as painful as you thought it would be. There are many tools that help with this, such as rate escalators in your retirement plan to increase your contribution amount each year and automatic bill pay. The more you do this, the happier you will be.

Whenever we discuss money, somewhere along the way, greed and envy will come into play. Unfortunately, these shortcomings can impair your ability to make good investment decisions. In his famous book

Manias, Panics, and Crashes, economic historian Charles P. Kindleberger said, "There is nothing so disturbing to one's well-being and judgment as to see a friend get rich."[7]

When you see people around you finding success with their money, you may invest to keep up with them at your own peril, even if it means investing money well beyond your comfort zone. Talking it over with a financial coach to gain proper perspective will help you avoid these age-old behaviors.

Spatial Disorientation

Investor behavior can be more fully understood by comparing it to piloting an aircraft. If you understand how to pilot an aircraft, then you know the term *six-pack* doesn't refer to Budweiser or a popular new microbrew. Instead, six-pack refers to the six basic flight instruments. The three static instruments are airspeed indicator, altimeter, and vertical speed indicator. The three gyroscopic instruments include attitude indicator, heading indicator, and turn coordinator.

On a clear day, a pilot can see the horizon and adjust the aircraft accordingly. But visibility starts to crumble when clouds, thunderstorms, or fog present themselves, and now the pilot must solely rely on instruments.

Editor's note: If you live on the West Coast of the United States, you may refer to fog as the marine layer because you might be unwilling to admit that you live in a foggy city.

When human beings are not able to rely on their eyes to know which way is up, they use their ears. In many circumstances, while piloting a plane with poor visibility, a person's eyes and ears can begin to disagree as to what is up, down, right, and left. The results can be nothing short of catastrophic. This phenomenon is called spatial disorientation, and its effects are fatal 90 percent of the time.[8] The most famous recent occurrence of spatial disorientation was in 1997; John F. Kennedy Jr., his wife, and his sister-in-law died in a tragic plane crash when he was piloting on their way to a family wedding.[9]

When you look at the charts and their descriptions on the next few pages, you need to remember that these are the facts that your eyes are reading off of your cockpit instruments. Sometimes, though, your ears (your gut instinct) will tell you that it is a permanent loss and not a temporary correction. If you trust your ears instead of your eyes, your portfolio will have a fatal crash. If you end up trusting your gut most of the time, then you have to have a financial coach to remain on course.

When you witness a turbulent time in the stock market, do you see it as mere volatility that presents a wonderful buying opportunity? Or, conversely, do you believe it is a disaster that you just lost that money and think you should sell to cut your losses? If you see the disaster scenario, then you are suffering spatial disorientation as an investor. Take a look at these charts, and we'll explain what you're up against. First, we'll begin with what we'll call the "Percentages of Probability" chart.

Risk of Stock Market Loss over Time

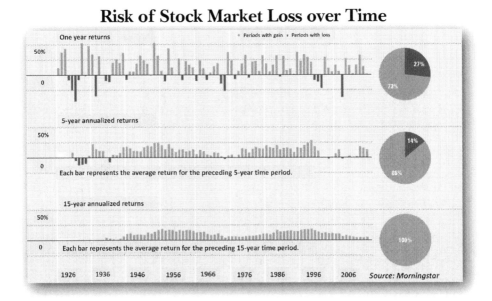

Source: Morningstar

Pretend you're walking down the street in Las Vegas and come across a wheel game. The gentleman running the game explains that when you spin the wheel, you will win seven out of ten times. Will you play? We think you will. That is exactly what the chart above shows, except it is not Las Vegas. Rather, it's the one-year returns for the S&P 500 from 1926 to 2015.

History demonstrates that 73 percent of the time, the stock market is in the positive and negative only 27 percent of the time. Those are pretty great odds in or out of Las Vegas. We'll take winning 73 percent of the time anytime.

It gets even better if you look at five-year rolling periods instead of mere one-year timeframes. This shows the S&P 500 is positive 86 percent of the time and only negative 14 percent of the time. We like that the odds are getting better. Now look at the fifteen-year timeframe. What you see is that the market is up 100 percent of the time.

Let that sink in: 100 percent of the time, the S&P 500 is up over a fifteen-year period going all the way back to 1926. That includes during the crash of 1929, the ensuing Great Depression, World War Two, JFK's assassination, Vietnam, Watergate, 1970's Stagflation, gasoline lines, 1987's Black Monday, the Gulf War, the late 1990's tech bubble, 9/11, the Iraq War, and finally 2008's bailouts and Great Recession.

Amazingly, even with every stumbling block imaginable, the stock market, as measured by the S&P 500 over a fifteen-year period, has never been negative. Even in the short term, it is up three out of every four years. And when it is up, it is actually up quite a bit.

Stocks, Bonds, Bills, and Inflation 1926-2015

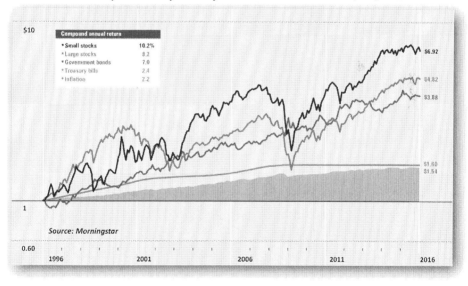

We are willing to bet that you'd sit down at the craps table in Las Vegas if you were going to win three out of every four rolls. But here's where emotions creep in. If you sit there gambling long enough, the odds say you'll lose two rolls in a row eventually—or maybe three or four rolls in a row, the dice could go cold. This is when it feels like the wheels have just completely fallen off, and you're mad you can't find a clock anywhere in the casino. At this point, the waitress can't bring the drinks fast enough.

From 1929 to 1932, the S&P 500 was negative four consecutive years. That hurts. From 1939 to 1941, it was down three years in row. It was down twice in a row in 1973 to 1974 and thrice from 2000 to 2002. If you're keeping score at home, you know that the second-worst year ever was 2008, when the S&P 500 dropped a whopping 37 percent. But it is those consecutive negative years that can really rock you with a prolonged sense of doubt about whether your money is invested in the right places.

Average Investor vs. S&P 500

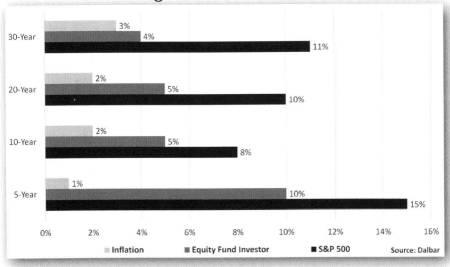

Due to uncertainty, doubt, and fear, individual investors dramatically underperform the stock market because they act on those concerns. In many years, investment companies have more money being pulled out of mutual funds than is being invested when the market declines. In other words, investors are fleeing the market after they have lost value.

The above chart shows that over a twenty-year period, the S&P 500 averaged 9.85 percent annually, while the average equity investor during the same time only did a disappointing 5.19 percent. That's a 4.66 percent difference. We think it's a concerning number. That's a lot of risk and gut-ache for only a 5.19 percent annual rate of return. It is even worse when you look at the thirty-year numbers.

This is why we said earlier that our "Swipe Left Law of Investing" reads, "For every action, there is an equal and opposite reaction; or maybe not." The equal and opposite reaction in a purely emotionless world would be to invest more money to take advantage of a price decrease, much like buying more food when it is on sale. Alas, we do not live with Spock on Vulcan and react that way.

So, when does a 0.15 percent management fee cost an investor 4.66 percent? Yes, we asked that question correctly, even though it does not sound like it would make any sense. The truth is that if an investor merely chases the lowest fees, but buys and sells at the wrong time, it doesn't matter how low the fee is when the actual performance turns out to be awful because of bad behavior. Hence, a 0.15 percent fee here actually effectively costs the investor 4.66 percent. Don't believe us? Well, just read that previous paragraph again; the numbers don't lie.

Asset-class returns 1996-2015

Asset Class	Average Annual Return (%)	Standard Deviation (%)
Large Cap Value	8.5%	15.2%
Large Cap Core	8.2%	15.3%
Small Cap	8.8%	19.9%
Large Cap Growth	7.6%	17.5%
Diversified Portfolio	7.4%	10.0%
Fixed Income	5.3%	3.5%
International	4.4%	16.7%
Cash	2.5%	0.7%

Source: Income Investment Solutions

One of the ways to mitigate that roller-coaster feeling is to invest your money in such a way that you still have a solid average annual return, but your dips are less frequent and not as steep. This chart shows a strategy using a well-diversified portfolio returning nearly identical performance to large-cap stocks in general, but with significantly less volatility.

An easy way to think about volatility is by using a weather analogy. Did you know that Dallas, Texas, and San Diego, California, both have average daily temperatures of sixty-four degrees? It was a surprise to us as well. We assumed Dallas was much hotter, but it's not. They both average out to a pleasant sixty-four degrees.

The difference is Dallas turns into an inferno during the summer months and is known for epic heat waves. In fact, 2011 saw forty days in a row of heat in excess of one hundred degrees. During the winter months, Dallas has its share of below-freezing temperatures and ice storms. Meanwhile, San Diego usually peaks in the upper seventies and bottoms out in the low forties on its very worst days.

The question then becomes, do you want to live with radical temperature swings of above a hundred degrees to below freezing, or do you want to live with modest, comfortable swings from the seventies to the forties, where a light sweater is the equivalent of a heavy coat?

In a nutshell, that's volatility. The weather in San Diego is much less volatile than in Dallas. It is more emotionally comfortable if you have less volatility. If market downturns make you nervous, then it is best to avoid an investment portfolio that needs both excessive sunscreen application and a heavy winter coat.

Editor's note: the TV show *Dallas* gave us J. R. Ewing while *Three's Company* (set in Southern California) gave us Jack Tripper and Mr. Furley, so maybe don't base where you'll live solely on weather patterns.

Asset-Class Winners and Losers 1996-2015

	1996	1997	1998	1999	2000	2001	2002	2003	2004	2005	2006	2007	2008	2009	2010	2011	2012	2013	2014	2015
Highest Return	23.0	33.4	28.5	20.9	21.5	22.8	17.8	60.7	20.7	14.0	26.9	11.6	26.9	32.5	31.3	27.1	18.2	45.1	24.7	1.4
	17.8	22.8	28.3	27.3	9.9	7.8	1.6	39.2	18.4	7.8	16.2	9.8	1.6	28.1	16.1	2.9	17.9	32.4	13.7	0.0
	10.2	15.6	13.1	21.0	0.1	3.7	-6.3	28.7	11.9	7.1	15.8	5.5	-17.9	26.5	13.0	2.1	16.0	23.3	7.4	-0.4
	6.4	15.9	11.9	14.3	-3.6	-0.6	-13.3	26.2	14.9	5.7	13.0	5.2	-36.7	14.4	10.1	0.0	11.1	17.6	2.9	-0.8
	5.2	5.3	4.9	4.7	-9.1	-11.9	-15.7	1.4	8.5	4.9	4.8	4.7	-37.0	0.1	6.2	-3.3	2.4	0.0	0.0	-0.7
Lowest Return	-0.9	2.1	-7.3	-8.0	-14.0	-21.2	-22.1	1.0	3.3	3.0	1.2	-5.2	-43.1	-14.9	0.1	-11.7	0.1	-12.8	-4.5	-3.6

○ Small stocks ○ Large stocks ○ International stocks ○ Long-term government stocks ○ Treasury bills ○ Diversified Portfolio

Source: Morningstar

Diversification and asset allocation are going to be significant players in helping you minimize volatility. Diversification is when you own multiple investments while asset allocation is when you own assets across different sectors of the economy. You have all heard the saying, "Don't put all your eggs in one basket." Instead of only owning General Electric (GE) and then saying, "OK, I'm fine on large cap now because I have GE in my portfolio," you want to own lots of investments in each asset class. Most people find it more efficient to do so using mutual funds, ETFs, or variable-annuity subaccounts.

Diversification will spread out your risk and can reduce overall investing stress, especially if you are using an indexing strategy. This should contribute to lower volatility and make the ride smoother. Significant market declines are normal even if you are diversified, as we learned in 2008.

Don't let worry and fear get the better of you, though. The historical record is that upturns have followed downturns. This is a fact that has awarded long-term investors with billions of dollars of wealth creation in the preceding decades. Remember, though, that the upturns outpace the downturns both in frequency and returns.

Some asset classes correlate well together, and others do not. Correlation is just a fancy way of saying that each asset class performs differently at different times for distinct reasons. Think of the shocks on your car; they individually adjust for the bump at each wheel. The chart above illustrates how a well-diversified and allocated portfolio can smooth out the crests and troughs of the market. You can see that you may not get the maximum returns in any given year, but you will consistently perform well above the lowest-performing asset class.

A good financial coach will develop an asset-allocation model for you that will match your long-term investment goals as well as your temperament. There are many asset classes, and they can be defined in numerous ways. You don't need to know everyone. But the more asset classes you have exposure to in your portfolio, the smoother the ride should be.

It does help to know some of the more common areas, though. We will start with growth and value. A growth stock may be more aggressive and appreciate more, while a value stock may pay higher dividends for income seekers.

It's helpful to know that "large cap" means big company stocks like Microsoft and Ford Motor Co., whereas "mid cap" and "small cap" are smaller companies that perhaps you haven't heard of yet. Then you also have international, emerging markets, real estate, commodities, and utilities. On the bond side, there are fixed income, government, corporate, long-term, short-term, high yield (these were once called junk bonds in the 1980s, but now they have a fancier name), and convertibles. A proper asset-allocation model will make sure that you are able to participate in the upside of each asset class when it is performing well.

Determinants of Portfolio Performance

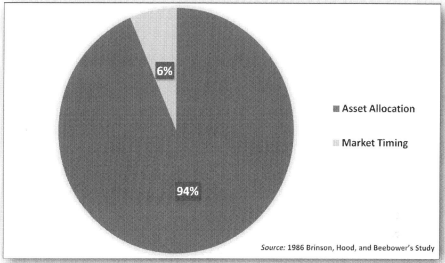

Asset Allocation

Market Timing

6%

94%

Source: 1986 Brinson, Hood, and Beebower's Study

On a different note, we are going to let you in on a little secret, which we alluded to earlier. Here it is: Market timing does not work. It has never worked. Oh, in the short term it seems like it works, much like everyone you know wins in Vegas, but over the long term it does not work.

Even with the most sophisticated and powerful computers in the history of the world, it is not possible to know exactly what is going to happen next or with what magnitude. The funny part is that the reason that you can't know what the price of any one stock or bond might do is that there is a human element tied into it. See, you are not alone in making behavioral decisions.

The markets are driven by emotional responses, and yet nobody can accurately predict how any given segment of the human population will actually behave on any given day. Factors for why we do what we do can come down to how hot or cold the weather is, and we all know how well we predict the weather! It isn't wrong to try to maximize your performance results. However, it is wrong to try to achieve those maximized results through market timing. It is still a fool's errand. In order to maximize performance results, investing must be done in a comprehensive manner.

The Cost of Market Timing 1996-2015

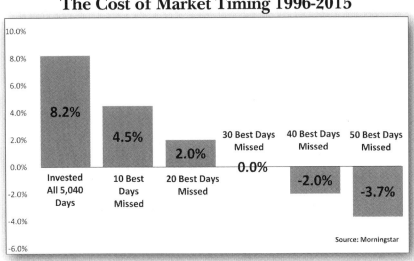

This chart shows the significance of remaining invested through both good times and bad times. From 1996 to 2015, if you had merely missed the ten best-performing days out of 5,040, you would have had a gigantic difference in your return. Staying invested those best ten days would have earned you 82 percent more money. See what we mean?

You can't predict and time the market because you would have to not miss one of those ten days. The performance numbers get exponentially worse the more days that you miss. If you'd sat out just the best twenty days out of 5,040, you'd have forfeited almost 310 percent of all the gains in the market.

One of us spent time consulting for a third-party dynamic and tactical asset money manager. After seeing this role from the inside, we can declare that if you see those words together describing your asset manager, then you should run away fast. It is a strategy based on market timing that argues that a quantitative computer algorithm can predict what asset class you should be in at any given time.

Are your eyes crossed yet? A classic example of this failing money-management strategy is the recent implosion in 2015 of the multibillion-dollar Curian Capital Management. By the way, if you try to look them up, you will find that they don't exist anymore.

Most of these third-party dynamic and tactical asset money managers charge 1 percent in addition to the advisor's 1 percent fee and on top of the cost of the underlying investments, which can easily put the client's total expense in the 3 to 4 percent range. That is awfully pricey to not outperform most index funds. Ironically, there are even some variable annuities with guaranteed living and death benefits cheaper than that.

Many third-party money managers are selling the falsehood, usually for a performance-killing, high management fee, that they can predict the right asset class at the right time. The truth is that when a terrorist attack happens, those algorithms have no idea what is going to happen next or how investors will emotionally react during the following day's trading. It is sort of like when in *The Wizard of Oz*, the little dog Toto runs over and bites the pant leg of the wizard behind the curtain. The audience then sees that it is a game of smoke and mirrors with a high fee attached.

They like to use lots of fancy phrases like "persistency in price," and "risk-adjusted implementation," or "drills down by platform," attempting to add credibility to their methodology. One of the misleading things these types of managers do is the way they present historical performance data to potential investors. They show back-tested and walk-forward numbers instead of actual performance data.

When they don't like what the performance history shows, they simply rewrite their quantitative money-management algorithm to make it look better. Then they apply the new algorithm to historical market data and show the client how the new algorithm would have performed. However, as an investor, you care how it *actually performed* or will perform.

Unfortunately, that information is mysteriously hidden. It is a huge risk to investors and a significant oversight that securities regulators allow clients to only be shown back-tested and walk-forward performance numbers. At the end of the day, it is nearly impossible to know if they are real or imagined.

When should an investor consider that paying higher fees for active management might be a good value? One example is municipal-bond funds. One of the major risks with bonds is default risk. Simply put, the bond issuer might not be solvent when it is time to repay the bond's principal.

Index-bond funds don't screen for default risk. They buy all the bonds in the pertinent index. So, do you want a cheaper index-bond fund that doesn't screen for higher risk or would you rather pay a marginally higher fee to invest in a bond fund that significantly reduces the risk of default? We think this could be a plausible time to pay a higher fee because you receive great value and decreased risk.

Real Rate of Return after Taxes and Inflation

Year	CD Rate	Taxes	Inflation	Real Rate of Return
2005	3.73%	28.0%	3.40%	-0.71%
2006	5.24%	28.0%	3.20%	0.57%
2007	5.23%	28.0%	2.85%	0.91%
2008	3.14%	28.0%	3.85%	-1.59%
2009	0.87%	28.0%	-0.34%	0.97%
2010	0.44%	28.0%	1.64%	-1.32%
2011	0.42%	28.0%	3.16%	-2.86%
2012	0.63%	28.0%	2.10%	-1.65%
2013	0.50%	28.0%	1.20%	-1.56%
2014	0.65%	28.0%	1.30%	-0.83%

Sources: CDA Weisenberger, Federal Reserve Board, and InflationData.com

As promised, we are hitting you with a ton of data in this chapter. It will be worth it, though. Let's take a quick a moment and put the numbers in context to better understand another risk you face. When we are talking about "Grow It," we don't only mean you are pushing for a larger account value tomorrow.

Specifically, we mean that you are increasing your purchasing power over time. More purchasing power translates to being able to buy more with your money tomorrow than you can today. This means you must not only outpace inflation, but you can't let taxes beat you, either. Inflation historically tracks around 3 percent annually, and you can see in the chart above where taxes stand. That is no small task. Net of all expenses, taxes, and inflation, you have to do much better than 3 percent to keep up. Do you see the dilemma if you are starting out at a 2 percent return and then need to subtract everything else?

One of the biggest errors we see investors make is that they confuse safety with certainty. Safety means not losing money. As we just said, money is your purchasing power. Therefore, a safe investment will preserve your purchasing power relative to other investments. And remember, the only way to preserve purchasing power is to outpace inflation.

Certainty means you know exactly what you have. Yet, just because you know what you have does not mean it is safe. Let's look at an example: Your CD at the bank paid you 1 percent last year, but inflation was 2 percent. Your money was absolutely certain since you knew to the penny exactly what was going to be in your account next year, but was your money safe? Nope, not even close.

You guaranteed yourself to lose money last year. You made 1 percent, and your account balance grew a little, but inflation was double that, meaning you actually lost purchasing power. Your $100,000 making 1 percent won't buy you as much this year as it did last year. That can't be considered safe by any definition, especially if compounded over numerous years.

The safest investments are those that have historically outpaced inflation and preserved or even expanded purchasing power. Unfortunately for people who gravitate toward certainty instead of safety, inflation and taxes don't take a sabbatical just because you're nervous. Only your mom loves you that much. Inflation doesn't care who you are.

Let's continue this idea by briefly returning to the spatial-disorientation discussion. You're reading this plethora of stock-market data, and all of your cockpit instruments are flashing red. They are unequivocally reporting that if you desire safety, you must be invested in equities. Otherwise, your portfolio is both doomed to certainty and certainly doomed.

However, you still don't feel good about what your instruments are spitting out. You are reading this book, and you are perhaps acknowledging that stock-market investing just doesn't fit your temperament. Give yourself a pat on the back for being honest.

We have seen that for many people, because of their temperaments, investing in the stock market is more akin to jumping out of an airplane than anything else. Imagine yourself going skydiving for the very first time. You get strapped together with your instructor, and he tells you it's about time to jump. You notice he's got one big parachute for the both of you, so you ask, "What if it doesn't open? Can I have a second backup parachute? That one might not open, either. Is it possible to have a third parachute? Then I will be ready to jump."

For many successful investors, simply having a talented financial coach put together a well-diversified portfolio is the only parachute needed. Others, like the person in this skydiving story, will only invest in the stock market if they know with certainty that all their money is guaranteed if they live and it is all guaranteed if they die.

They want a second and third parachute. Those extra parachutes aren't free, and they don't come cheaply. But the guarantees are available in the marketplace, and even with the extra fees, they may help you outpace inflation infinitely better than a fixed annuity or CD.

In this situation, an investor might decide to look at a variable annuity with additional guarantees as a multiparachute option. You should know that variable annuities are a major hot-button area within the financial-services industry. There is little gray area with variable annuities. Nearly every financial professional has a strong opinion.

Some opinions are glowing, and others are glaring. But we've learned that these professionals' opinions, good or bad, are based on their own biases instead of based upon the client's temperament. If you read something negative about variable annuities, there is a high probability that the author is attacking the product because of surrender charges, commissions, or fees. These are valid concerns, because when you include those extra parachutes, they can become real pricey, real quick.

The flip side, though, as we have discussed, is that investing for certainty instead of growth doesn't get you where you need to be. Depending on your particular needs and personality, using a variable annuity can be either really good or really bad. If your investing behavior requires you to have extra parachutes, you will still be much better off, net of fees.

So, who would be the person that would require the use of a variable annuity? If you are someone that invests in mutual funds and ETFs, but your emotions dictate very poor buy-and-sell decisions, or if you are anchored to CDs and fixed annuities because of fear, then those variable annuity fees are probably worth every penny. Otherwise, if you do not match those descriptions, then a good financial coach will find you a more cost-effective way to invest.

If you don't like variable annuities but still need additional parachutes, then you might try a collar strategy using put options and covered-call options with your stock portfolio. In 2013, Joe Tomlinson wrote an interesting research article entitled "The Best Solution for Protecting Retirement Portfolios: Put and Call Options versus GLWBs [Guaranteed Living Withdrawal Benefits]."

For investors who don't want to invest in the stock market without significant downside protection, he compared the additional cost of the variable annuity with the additional expenses associated with buying and selling options on a 65 percent stock portfolio and a 35 percent bond portfolio. The results were surprising, and they showed a stripped-down, low-fee variable annuity was less expensive than an option-heavy stock portfolio.

Conversely, the option-heavy stock portfolio was less expensive than a higher-fee, higher-surrender-charge variable annuity.[10] There are several plausible strategies for an investor to get equities exposure with downside protection that can be worth paying higher fees to implement and manage. The essential point here that you cannot miss is that you need exposure to equities. Get in equities somehow, and use whatever strategy lets you sleep at night.

Surely someone reading this book is old enough that they remember the 1929 stock-market crash and the ensuing Great Depression. We understand that we may not be able to convince that person to go into equities. That's OK. Regardless, whether or not you go into equities, you will still need plenty of retirement income.

If you won't invest to earn 10 percent a year and instead invest to earn 2 percent a year, then you must understand that your behavior isn't about stock-market discipline; it is about budgeting and saving more. If you earn 2 percent instead of 10 percent, then you will need to save significantly more to reach the same retirement income goal. As we talked about in "Plan It," you need a plan, so plan for a much larger savings rate.

Besides investing for certainty, another glaring misplacement of investment priorities is focusing on account balances. It's human nature to want to look at your 401(k) or IRA account statements and hope that the dollar amount is growing. The bigger the dollar amount, the more money you have.

But when you're saving and growing your money, you should be focusing on the number of shares in your account, not the actual dollar figure. We know that sounds a little counterintuitive. Over a lifetime of investing, the way to create significant wealth is to accumulate as many stock, mutual fund, or ETF shares as possible. The next few charts will explain how to best complete a share-accumulation strategy.

Dollar Cost Averaging

Contributions	Investment Amount	Share Price	Shares Purchased
1	$200	$50	4
2	$200	$40	5
3	$200	$20	10
4	$200	$40	5
Totals:	$800	$150	24

- Average share price of the four contributions: $150/4 = $37.50
- Participant's cost per share: $800/24 = $33.33

Source: My Federal Retirement http://www.myfederalretirement.com/public/363.cfm

Two excellent behaviors geared toward maximizing performance and accumulating more shares are dollar-cost averaging (DCA) and rebalancing. DCA helps put the focus on buying shares. If you invest in your 401(k), then you're already using DCA to go into your investment choices.

Every Friday when you get paid, you are deferring a set percentage of your compensation, and you're buying shares. If the market is down that Friday, then you are buying more shares because they are cheaper. If the market is up that Friday, then you are purchasing fewer shares because they are more expensive.

These "down" days, or weeks, or months in the market are buying opportunities. Over time you should get the cheapest average price per share because you are buying fewer at higher prices and more at lower prices. To keep it simple, in the DCA chart above, we are using a modest $200 a month for a mere four months. This shows that you would have an average cost savings of $4.17 per share. Successfully using DCA over time can add enough extra shares to your portfolio to build an extra few hundred thousand dollars, and who doesn't need a little more cash at retirement?

OK, pause to take a deep breath. Now, one more time, go back and spend a few moments looking at the DCA chart again. Did you notice, we mean really notice, that as the price of the investment goes down, you are able to buy more shares?

I know in the abstract we all understand that if something at Target or Walmart is on sale, then that's a good thing, and it means you get to buy more of whatever it is you want. However, to be a successful investor, you must grasp this inherent truth: when the market drops, then that means every one of those stocks, mutual funds, or ETFs that you need to buy so you can retire someday just went on sale.

A real-life example would be if you take a look at your 401(k) statements. You'll see how much money you made (or lost) that quarter, and you'll probably be happy if you see that the dollar amount grew. Next take a look at a quarterly statement where you had great performance and compare it with a quarterly statement where you had poor performance. Check out the number of shares you purchased in each of those quarters.

During your worst-performing quarters, you accumulated the largest number of additional shares for your portfolio. More shares means more value. Considering that fact in the proper perspective will help you accept that natural volatility benefits you in retirement accounts during the "Grow It" stage.

Now we shift gears to discuss rebalancing. No matter what commodity or item you are talking about, the way to make a profit on it is to sell it for more than you bought it, right? Right! You want to buy low and sell high.

Rebalancing is a way to capture your gains and, believe it or not, outperform your actual investments by consistently selling your winners and using those gains to buy into the losers. In other words, you are automatically and repeatedly selling high and buying low.

Let's look at your portfolio's asset allocation and assume you had a hypothetical chart like this one.

Portfolio Rebalancing

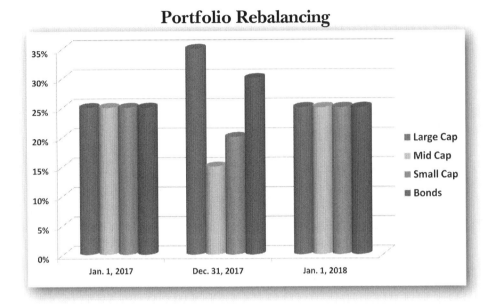

Keeping it simple, the first bar chart shows that on January 1, 2017, you have 25 percent each in large cap, mid cap, small cap, and bonds.

The second bar chart shows on December 31, 2017, how your portfolio performed throughout the year. Large cap went up the most, mid cap declined the most, small cap declined a little, and bonds went up some. The third bar chart shows the portfolio rebalancing so that on January 1, 2018, you have 25 percent equally weighted once again to your original portfolio recommendation.

Rebalancing has several huge benefits. First, you know that each year your portfolio will go back to your appropriate risk profile, so you never get too conservative or too aggressive for your own comfort level. Second, the various asset classes do well at different times—remember, low correlation helps.

In order to rebalance, you have to sell what went up the most and reinvest in either what did not go up as much or in what went down a little. You might be thinking, "Wait a minute—I think you idiots just advised me to sell my winners and buy more of my losers." Yes, we did.

Asset classes perform cyclically. If you don't believe us, just refer back to the asset class box chart and see how they perform at different times. We urge you to sell high and buy low and then repeat that process annually.

Third, as we said just a minute ago, rebalancing allows you to outperform your actual investments. If you buy large cap low and sell it high, buy small cap low and sell it high, and so on, then you are constantly locking in your gains and buying another asset class when it goes on sale. Continuously buying different asset classes on sale helps lead to this outperformance.

Finally, rebalancing will matter more when you're talking about bigger dollar amounts. Remember, when you stop systematically investing in a particular account, then you're no longer taking advantage of DCA. In this situation, rebalancing is an absolute necessity.

You can use a specific date to rebalance, as in our example. You can typically rebalance on a monthly, quarterly, semiannual, or annual basis as well. Another option you can use is to rebalance once your original percentages get beyond a certain point. For example, if you start at 25 percent and it goes to 30 percent, that is when you might have it rebalance.

We are not arguing one is better than the other. The point is that you want to make sure your original allocation does not get too far out of whack. A good financial coach will make sure you are using one of these methods.

A History of Declines

Type of Decline	Average Frequency	Average Length	Last Occurrence
-5% or more	About 3 times a year	47 days	August 2015
-10% or more	About once a year	115 days	August 2015
-15% or more	About once every 2 years	216 days	October 2011
-20% or more	About once every 3 ½ years	338 days	March 2009

Source: https://www.americanfunds.com/individual/planning/market-fluctuations/past-market-declines.html

Historically, when the stock market goes on sale, it is only temporary. This chart shows the average recovery times following sizeable stock-market corrections. It takes about forty-seven days on average to recover from a 5 percent drop, and a recent occurrence of this was in August 2015. A 10 percent drop happens about once a year and requires 115 days to bounce back on average. This also happened in August 2015.

Moving up to larger market drops, we see that a 15 percent down-swing typically needs around two years to recover, and an example of this happening was in October 2011. An actual bear market, which is a 20 percent or greater plunge, happens approximately once every three and a half years and takes 338 days on average to recoup those losses. Such a large slump happened in March 2009, following the Great Recession.

US Market Recovery after Financial Crisis

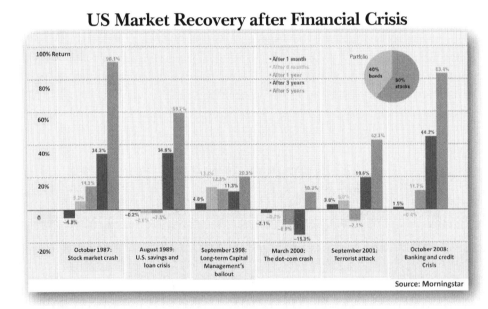

Source: Morningstar

These are sales, and they only last for so long. It doesn't matter whether it is a grocery store, car dealership, fitness center, or the stock market that is offering the sale. In every single instance, the buyer pays less. If you are fifty years old and have fifteen more years before you retire, then you should not only embrace a temporary market sale—you should look forward to it. It means you are going to accumulate that many more shares than you would have if the price just went straight up from the moment you started investing.

Remember a few pages ago when we were talking about how average investors let emotions drive their decision-making, thereby hurting their performance? Selling your shares after there's been a meaningful correction or drop in prices because you get scared and then buying back in when prices go back up after you feel safe means you just sold pretty low and bought back in fairly high. Even just one huge and poorly timed decision like that can wipe out an entire lifetime of disciplined DCA investing through your paychecks. Ouch!

Summary

During your investing life, there will be wild and unexpected swings in overall market conditions and even within your own portfolio. There may be times when you want to sell everything and put your money under the mattress or buy gold as a safe harbor. But before you do, always remember the question you should be asking yourself: "Is this just a temporary change in the market, or did my retirement goals actually change?"

Let's ask that question one more time, just to hammer home the point. "Is this just a temporary change in the market, or did my financial goals actually change?" Once you respond to that question by almost always answering correctly that your financial goals have not in fact changed, then it's time to focus like a laser on getting it right.

Getting it right means two things. First, eliminate the Swipe Left Law of Investing, "For every action, there is an equal and opposite reaction; or maybe not." Second, enact the Swipe Right Law of Investing for yourself: "When designing a portfolio, the focus should be on how you emotionally respond to stock-market facts and events."

Your goal is to "Grow It." You are going to need your portfolio's performance to keep up with the stock market and beat inflation. Do not forget that this need requires you to choose an investment strategy that will give you the courage to trust your cockpit instruments. We hope that by this point you realize that even though it is possible to do this all on your own, much like flying a plane, it does not necessarily make the most sense.

At many points in our lives, we need someone to be there to help us stay the course and have the courage to do the right thing despite what our guts are telling us. Sometimes we need that calm voice of reason. When it comes to investing, that calm voice will be your financial coach.

CHAPTER 3

PROTECT IT

We should be careful to get out of an experience only the wisdom that is in it and stop there lest we be like the cat that sits down on a hot stove lid. She will never sit down on a hot stove lid again, and that is well, but also she will never sit down on a cold one anymore.
—MARK TWAIN, NINETEENTH-CENTURY AMERICAN WRITER AND SATIRIST

Think back to the first car you owned. It was probably decent but not the newest model. It probably had several dents and scratches, the paint was a little faded, and it used oil as fast as gas. One positive was that it was paid for. Another positive was that you didn't need much insurance.

As time goes on and incomes go up, you buy better cars and better insurance. You buy better auto insurance mainly because you have no choice. State laws, lenders, and property-insurance agents all make sure you are properly covered.

Unfortunately, if left on your own, you probably would not be as diligent. How do we know this? All you have to do is look at how you don't leverage other insurance to protect common risks. We will tackle several behaviors in this chapter that, if not properly handled, would have you owning a 2017 Mercedes lifestyle with the protection of a 1982 Datsun.

Have you ever said, "That will never happen to me," or, "Sure, that happens, but I have nothing to worry about?" If so, welcome to being normal. Various factors influence how we perceive risk.

Women, as arguably the wiser half of our population, see risk much more readily than men. Older people recognize it more than the young, and the better educated you are, the more awareness you possess. Even if you are a well-educated older woman, you still struggle with mental blocks that keep you from properly addressing an exposed backside.

For almost all of us, our experience with insurance has caused us to view it through the lens of an unenjoyable line item in our budgets. Mistakenly categorizing insurance as an expense might make you miss the true value that it can provide. Think of it this way—insurance provides a cost-effective way to guarantee future security.

The trick is that you never know if you will need the future payment or not. This uncertainty causes many people to struggle with discerning if this expense is worthwhile when compared to the value being provided. Trying to balance those ideas is understandable, but keep in mind that cost is only an issue in the absence of value.

How each one of us perceives value is the catch. We could argue that a high-priced luxury car is of little value if all you care about is getting from point A to point B. Others could argue that if you have to spend time in a car, it should be as luxurious as possible. Both are true, depending on where you place value. With that in mind, you will have to decide if the benefit that can be provided is worth the cost. In other words, don't buy any kind of insurance because it is cheap; buy it because it adequately covers your risk.

Another mentality you need to be aware of is in properly understanding short-term versus long-term planning. If you have a long-term need, such as estate planning, and try to solve it with a short-term solution, you will consistently miss your goal. Not only will you miss your goal, you will end up paying a much higher premium to fix your problem.

As an example, we have a mutual friend, Brian, who loves to hike yet tends to buy cheap hiking boots that he has to replace about every other year. Russ, on the other hand, bought a very expensive pair that he has owned for almost a decade. If we do a cost analysis, it soon becomes clear that by focusing on the short term (Brian didn't want to pay $250 for boots), Brian actually cost himself more both in money and comfort. We do this all the time with insurance.

We convince ourselves that we can go cheaper. If paying less today is your goal, then be ready to pay more down the road. The fact of life is that you will pay something. We have found when you try to pay less today, it almost always will cost you more later.

Consider for a minute what you do for a living. If you have done it for a long time or it is a specialized area, you most likely consider yourself an expert on the subject. That is a wonderful thing, but don't let that allow you to believe you are an expert in all areas of life. Remember the example we gave in the last chapter about doctors and their retirement plans? This expert attitude manifests itself in the form of designing a plan on your own or removing options that might better solve your needs.

One coach we have known for years asks every new client if there are any products he should remove from his toolbox before he presents solutions. If they do mention a particular product, he always asks why. Many times, he uncovers outdated information or a misunderstanding of how that tool works. Other times he learns that a past experience is influencing the decision.

If you are seeking the most efficient solution to your problems, you have to keep all options on the table. No one would use a screwdriver to put a nail in a board, but if you dismiss an option as an "expert," a screwdriver might be all that is left to use.

Along these lines, it is easy to become focused on a product or tool and fail to see the purpose. Every year people go out and buy millions of drill bits. How many of those people wanted a drill bit? The answer is none, zero, zilch. What they wanted was a hole. If someone mentions permanent life insurance, do you cringe because when you were twenty-something, a friend of yours sold you an expensive life policy that you ended up canceling because it cost too much and you didn't see the benefit?

We get it. We have seen it happen too many times. The challenge, though, is to not let that error lead to another. At some point, more comprehensive life insurance might be the perfect solution. Unfortunately, you will never know if you allow a bias to develop that may no longer be pertinent.

Company Ratings

As a consumer, you need to be acutely aware of the financial stability of any insurance company you decide to do business with. The best way to evaluate a company's strength is by using one of the rating agencies listed in the chart below or by referring to the Comdex ratings. The reason this is necessary is because every time an insurance company issues a policy, it is making you a financial promise.

The likelihood of that company being able to keep that promise is directly correlated to its financial strength. Taking that into consideration, you should almost never partner with an insurance company with ratings below an A- or with a Comdex rating below 85. There are just so many high-quality companies from which to choose that going below those rating levels shouldn't be necessary. One exception to this rule is if you have a health condition or unique situation that can only be covered by a lower-rated company.

Rating Agencies

Credit Risk	Moody's	Standard and Poor's	Fitch Ratings
Investment grade	-----	-----	-----
Highest Quality	Aaa	AAA	AAA
High Quality	Aa1, Aa2, Aa3	AA+, AA, AA-	AA+, AA, AA-
Upper medium	A1, A2, A3	A+, A, A-	A+, A, A-
Medium	Baa1, Baa2, Baa3	BBB+, BBB, BBB-	BBB+, BBB, BBB-
Junk Grade	Ba1	BB+	BB+

Life Insurance

Insurance is a gigantic and, we will be honest here, dull topic. Not only do you have to look at each area (home, auto, health, life, disability, long-term care), you also have a myriad of options within each category. This discussion is rarely a simple conversation. To make it easier, we will focus on the main areas where you have some control and where the biggest risks (even if you don't see them) exist.

A great quality of eighteen-year-olds is that they never, ever, under any circumstance, think they are going to die. They are immortal, not to mention right about everything. As we get older, that concept of immortality slowly fades from our minds. Somewhere around middle age, we start to realize that maybe we do have an expiration date, but it is a long way off in the future.

This eighteen-year-old mind-set would be fine if it were anywhere close to being true. Sadly, people die every day. We see it on the news, so we know that it is true, but this is where our minds play a couple of tricks on us.

First, since we are watching it, that means it was someone else, not us. It is never us—well, until it is. Unfortunately, this mentality contributes to us leaving our loved ones behind with much less than we would probably want. We postpone taking the proper steps until we are either too old or too physically and mentally worn down.

The second challenge is that if we do momentarily accept our passing as being plausible, we fail to grasp how expensive we would be to replace. Consider a stay-at-home spouse. He or she brings in no income, so a traditional analysis might skip over his or her actual monetary value. In many cases, the cost to replace the child care, house maintenance, et cetera, could easily exceed $250,000 over a short period. Not a small amount for anyone.

Now assume we are talking about the primary wage earner. The general rule of thumb is to take someone's paycheck and multiply it by ten or twenty. This means that if you make $75,000 a year, then you would need between $750,000 and $1.5 million to replace the potential future income of that individual. That amount only works if there are no debts, the mortgage is paid off, college is funded, and retirement funds are maxed.

We don't know about you, but for most people, that is not very realistic. Regardless, let's carry out the scenario assuming no debt. In this case, $1.5 million generating income at 4 percent a year would mean an income of $60,000. That translates to $1,250 less each month for the surviving spouse. That might be enough if not for your goals and obligations.

For an example, let's look at the chart and case study below:

Case Study

Jimmy age 40   Sally age 38
Children: ages 8 and 10

Assets		Debts		Income
Home	$400,000	Mortgage	$250,000	$80,000
401(k)	$100,000	Home Equity Loan	$27,000	
College Funds	$30,000	Autos	$35,000	
Investments	$20,000	Credit Cards	$8,000	
Total:	$550,000	Total	$320,000	

Risk	Need	Death Benefit to Cover	20 year Term Cost	Permanent Cost (UL)
Income Replacement	$55,000 a year	$1,400,000	$95/month	$725/month
Debt	$320,000	$320,000	$28/month	$180/month
College Funding	$150,000	$150,000	$18/month	$104/month
Retirement Funding	$65,000	$65,000	$8/month	$45/month

Income replacement assumes debt and mortgage are paid off at death. Rate of return of assets to determine future needs assumed at 7%. College funding assuming 8 years at $20,000 a year. Life Insurance illustrated using Male age 40 in Colorado Preferred Non-Tobacco

Run through this exercise to see if what you have between work and personal life policies is enough. If we had to make a guess, we would say that you don't have enough. When surveys are done regarding the amount of life insurance the average American owns, there is a serious shortfall.

Part of the reason for this gap is what we have just discussed. An additional factor is what people are willing to pay. Nobody likes to pay for something they will never be able to enjoy. This reality makes it tempting for us to go cheap and challenging to see the full value.

As we were writing this book, we asked a couple of friends to read over it. Two of them are executives at a Fortune 100 company, and by all accounts they are well-educated and successful people. Once they finished this section, both admitted that they needed to review their current coverage as they were far short of what they required. It is important to get proper guidance on how to properly cover your needs. That will require you to sit down with someone to help determine both how much and what types of insurance will be best for you.

Hopefully, you are at the point of realizing the actual risk and are ready to determine the best way to cover it. When it comes to life insurance, the two main forms are term and permanent (which includes whole, universal, and variable). As you can see in the next chart, there are trade-offs with each type of policy.

Life-Insurance Comparison

	Term	Whole	Universal	Variable Universal
Premium	Guaranteed Level for term (i.e. 20 years).	Guaranteed Level.	Flexible or Guaranteed Level.	Flexible or Guaranteed Level.
Death Benefit	Temporary.	Guaranteed permanent.	Flexible, may increase or decrease.	Flexible, may increase or decrease.
Cash Value	None.	Yes, based on dividend payments. With a guaranteed minimum. Can change.	Yes, based on interest rates with a guaranteed minimum.	Yes, based on investment choices performance.
Advantages	Lowest premium for highest benefit.	Permanent benefit with guaranteed cash value.	Flexible premium and benefit.	Flexible premium and benefit. Higher cash value potential.
Disadvantages	Temporary benefit and premium guarantee.	High premium. Expenses not transparent.	Higher Premium.	Higher Premium. No cash value guarantees.

Term is less expensive, especially when you are younger. It becomes more expensive when you go to buy it as you age. This is because insurance companies have a solid handle on exactly what their risk is for any given group. They have been doing this for a long time, and they know when you will kick the bucket—well, statistically, that is. Term locks in the premium for a set number of years. It is possible to keep it after the term ends, but be prepared to pay astronomically higher rates.

Permanent policies last as long as you do, assuming you put in enough money. They have a cash-value component tied to the death benefit. Initially, you will pay much higher premiums compared to a term policy. Although, if these are done correctly, you should have some additional value in the form of cash accumulation, income tax benefits, estate planning, and liquidity. If you need to be insured for your entire life, permanent is usually the less-expensive option.

Cost Comparison of $500,000 Death Benefit

Male Issue Age:	20 Year Term Premium	Whole Life Premium	Whole Life Cash Value at 70	Universal
25	$27/month	$333/month	$407,742	$140/month
35	$29/month	$502/month	$378,854	$205/month
45	$60/month	$745/month	$292,201	$290/month
55	$150/month	$1,164/month	$208,290	$465/month
65	$490/month	$2,112/month	$88,024	$800/month
Illustrated preferred non-tobacco. Using A+ or better rated companies as of 12/16.	Premiums increase significantly year 21+.	Premiums stay level and build cash value.	Available to use for any need. Any value taken out will decrease the benefit in an equal amount.	Premiums stay level, no significant cash value.

We do apologize for the dull topic. Nevertheless, it is important as it plays into two other mentalities where you can go wrong.

One is the all-or-nothing approach. When you're young and starting off in your career with small children, term insurance is probably all you can afford, and it makes the most sense. As life goes on, expenses and liabilities will increase, such as having a mortgage.

Nothing drives us crazier than seeing a young adult with a small permanent life-insurance policy that doesn't cover his or her needs. Take a thirty-year-old that has done the exercise above and has determined he needs $1.8 million in coverage. If he buys a twenty-year term, his premium will be around $85 a month. For the same coverage in a stripped-down permanent policy at the lowest possible premium, it is $725. That is a crushing $643 a month extra expense. If he is on a tight budget and can only pay the $85 monthly, then he has two options.

The first option is to buy the term policy knowing he is properly covered. The second option is to reduce the permanent policy to a death benefit of $150,000 as that is all the $85 will buy. When you look at the two options, you probably realize there is only one right way.

So why do we even bring up the second option? Well, our experience is that many people have the wrong kind and amount of insurance. The culprit here is usually an insurance agent who was trained that permanent insurance is always the best type of insurance, as opposed to what fully covers the need.

Once you get into your fifties, you should have a very good idea of what your long-term insurance needs will be. If you have the proper term policies, you might be able to convert some of them into a permanent plan. One of the unintended consequences of being sold the wrong insurance at the wrong time is that when someone needs to upgrade his policy to match his needs, he won't because of the bad experience from when he was younger. All of this is not to say that permanent policies are bad. It is to say that you'd better make sure you are buying the proper drill bit for the hole you need.

As you move forward in life, you will still need some term insurance to adequately cover your risk and replace your income. The more you make, the more you have to replace. This does not mean that you should ignore some form of a permanent policy.

Along that same line, many people believe they will no longer need any form of life insurance once they get to a certain age or asset level. You will want to be cautious here as life can throw you a curveball. The irony of life is that the more successful you are in building your assets, the more you might need insurance after sixty-five. We will get into more depth on this subject in the "Leave It" chapter.

The second mentality to be aware of is a bias as to which form of insurance is better. This is a trap advisors fall into without ever realizing it. One of the jokes we used to say at one company was that whole life solved every problem—just ask home office. In fact, to them, whole life insurance was the Ginsu knife of the financial world.

They would tell you that it can be used as an emergency fund, a personal bank, future tax-free income, and a great death benefit when you pass away. It is true that it can do any one of those items mentioned, but what they forget to explain is that for every action, there is a reaction that diminishes how well the others work. If you want to hedge your bets, you can do it other ways with more efficiency.

Conversely, insurance agents joke about people who are termites. This refers to the idea that you only need to buy term insurance no matter what and invest the remainder. Great concept, but it rarely works. Most people fail to set aside the difference in premiums between permanent and term. They can very well end up needing a different form of insurance down the road, which will end up costing them more than if they had done proper planning. Both are ideas from which you should steer clear. Different types of policies provide leverage in different ways. In that same spirit, do not be the cat with the stove and dismiss a policy because it did not work in one environment or another.

An example of this is universal life, a permanent policy that grows the cash component based on current interest rates. If interest rates are high and then go down, like they did from 1990 to 2015, then the policy will not perform as illustrated. If, on the other hand, interest rates are low, like today, then the projections are probably close to the worst-case scenario. We know many people who will not use a universal life policy due to their past experiences, but that is ignoring the environment in which it was implemented. The same can be said for any form of insurance.

A financial coach will help you navigate these issues. There are new products and options coming out all the time. It is almost impossible to stay on top of what all the choices are and how they work in different scenarios. Not only will a financial coach know which type to use, but he or she will make sure you understand how it works and why it is an appropriate fit for you. If he or she can't do that, well, then you most likely are getting a pitch for a set of Ginsu knives you don't need.

You should make sure that, regardless of the type of insurance, your need has been clearly identified. From that point, you along with your financial coach can evaluate how best to meet that need. If you take a twenty-five-year-old with no children, no mortgage, and no debt, then life insurance is a very low priority in his or her financial world.

On the other hand, let's look at a forty-year-old. Assume he has three kids, is working on funding college, owes a mortgage, and has some credit card debt with no extra room in the budget. Say hello to a good-size term policy. Continuing through the stages of life, we will consider a seventy-year-old with a desire to leave a leveraged tax-free benefit behind. Now we have to shift over to a permanent policy that builds some cash value, but just enough to keep the policy in force. There are variations, of course—just make sure that the tool fits the project.

Disability

Throughout life everyone faces the risks of living too long, dying too early, or becoming physically impaired. When we are young, the first two rarely are a concern or even much of a risk, but the third is more common than people believe. The primary mind-set here is in still believing that it will never happen to us. Look at these statistics:

- Twenty-five percent of twenty-year-olds today will become disabled before they retire.[1]
- Over 37 million Americans are currently considered disabled, and over half of those are between the ages of 18 and 64.[2]
- In December 2012, there were 2.5 million people on Social Security Disability in their twenties, thirties, and forties.[3]

Think of it this way: What would happen if you found out today that your job ends tomorrow and that you have no hope of being employed in the next six to twelve months? Do you have enough money to pay your bills? What happens to your retirement planning when you can longer fund it and lose years of contributions? That is the reality of becoming disabled, since no one expects to become incapacitated.

So why don't more people have disability insurance? Several factors are in play. The first would be that many people get at least some kind of disability benefit from their employers. That is great if it is enough and can be transferred when you leave your employer. Many times, the benefit is capped or only covers a portion of the income needed. It also may be fully taxable.

If your gross monthly income is $7,000, then a 60 percent taxable benefit will net you $3,570. For most people, they will need closer to 80 percent of what they make to survive. If you have a disability that keeps you from working, there are most likely additional medical and rehabilitation costs. The purpose of any type of insurance is to make you whole. Therefore, 60 percent falls short, and you need at least 80 percent income replacement. If you are close to full Social Security age or have enough assets to sustain yourself for years, you can reduce that number. A key point is to never drop below 60 percent, no matter what.

Another challenge is that disability policies are not simple. There are multiple options that change or can be limited based on your occupation. A key point is that it needs to cover your workplace activity for what you specifically do. Make sure that you get a policy from a financially stable company that provides benefits to your full Social Security age, which for most people is now sixty-six to sixty-seven.

A good financial coach will know how to remove any gaps in your disability plan. A few questions to ask yourself include the following:

- Can I get by on Social Security disability with an average monthly benefit of $1,166?[4]
- Do I have any way to pay for extra medical costs, such as an HSA account?
- Can I do my job with some forms of disability, like vison impairment?
- Does my employer offer any additional disability insurance for a low cost?

For most people, the cost of coverage is usually affordable enough to provide you peace of mind. Again, a severe disability can put you out of control of your financial plan. It is at least worth a conversation with your financial coach to review any unnecessary exposure.

Long-Term Care

As you get older, you feel the effects of aging. Some days it is hard to remember where you left the keys or your phone. Heck, sometimes you are looking for the phone you are holding in your hand. Or maybe aging shows up in the physical sense as it gets harder to climb the stairs or as the recovery from a great workout takes longer than it used to. These are natural parts of aging.

Medical advancements have helped stretch out our life expectancies. They have also helped replace failing parts such as our hips and knees. What we don't and can't know is how much help we will need and when we might need that help. The odds are good that you will need long-term care; the question is how you plan to pay for that help.

How many people plan to pay for care based on what they believe are facts, but what are actually largely inaccurate assumptions? The biggest assumption is how long you will need help and how much it will cost you. It is easy to sit down and determine that statistically, the average person stays in a long-term care facility for thirty-six months, at an average cost of $6,800 per month.[5] This adds up to a total bill of $244,800.

You might decide that you can try to cover it with personal assets. The reason this assumption is dangerous is that you have no clue how much it will really cost. If you stay in a facility for twelve months, and the costs have risen due to increased demand, you might end up spending an additional $100,000.

Now, you might be thinking that you are never going to have to pay for long-term care. We hope you are right, but you just made the decision to pay for that care from your own pocket if it does happen. Be advised that self-insuring for that amount will draw blood and cause permanent scarring. You are effectively giving control away if you have no way to hedge your risk.

The second false assumption is that only you will be affected by not being prepared. Your children carry this burden right along with you financially, emotionally, and physically. Is your goal to leave something behind for your kids or grandkids? Do you want them to remember you as the person they had to bathe? Do you want them all to be close with one another after you are gone or angry that some stepped up while others disappeared at your time of need?

We ask because what happens for people that should be prepared but aren't is that they leave behind few assets to their exhausted and embattled heirs. If your goal is to leave behind pure chaos, then there's no need to hedge your bets. If not, then plan and leverage your resources today, so your kids and grandkids don't curse you in the grave.

The third faulty assumption is that it is too expensive to buy long-term care insurance. This misperception arises out of missing the value. If you see no value, any cost will be too great. Nobody wants to pay for something that they think they will never use. We are no different in that regard. Here is the issue: if you do need it and don't have it, there is little you can do to correct the situation.

With the above in mind, let's review what options are available to provide for long-term care assistance.

- Medicaid—here, you are depending on the state you live in to provide for your care. Due to the pressure put on Medicaid in recent years, you can hope to use this only if you are devoid of any assets outside of your home. Some states even have filial laws and are beginning to go back and sue children to recover expenses. These laws are a separate issue from the five-year look back on any transfer of assets. Here is the risk you run with this government-housing strategy; you don't get to pick which facility you are in, whether or not you have a roommate, or how long you will wait for an open bed.

- Family—if you have relatives nearby and your needs are limited, this might be a reasonable option. Our experience is that even though this is a cost-saving mechanism, it can take a severe emotional toll on family members. We know of many family members that no longer speak to one another after going through debilitating long-term care scenarios. In one client situation, a son had to provide all the care for his elderly father because his siblings lived too far away. During Thanksgiving one year, when the entire family was gathered together, the dad asked for an extra turkey leg. The son told him no. When it was mentioned to the son that he was perhaps a little too harsh considering the holiday occasion, he replied, "You don't have to lift him every time he goes to the bathroom, takes a bath, or goes to bed." This is the cruel reality of caring for an elderly parent.

- Self-Insuring—here, you set aside assets in case you have a need. The advantage is that you will not pay for something you don't ever use. The disadvantage is that you miss out on any leveraging. Also, you might be reducing any estate you plan on leaving behind.

- Traditional Long-Term-Care Insurance—this allows for the best way to leverage for long-term-care needs. One downside is that you have to pay an ongoing premium, and that premium can increase each year. This is what has been happening over the last several years. Another downside is you might be paying for something you never use.

- Linked-Benefit Policies—this is a relatively new development that allows you to hedge your bet. You can buy a life-insurance or annuity policy that has a long-term-care rider attached. This provides you the guarantee that the money will be used in the form of long-term-care benefits, a return of your premium, or a death benefit to your heirs. The trade-off is that you will get less leverage since you are making a policy do multiple things at once, but somebody will get back at least most, it not all, of what you put into the policy.

In this discussion, the main fork in the road is to either buy some form of long-term-care insurance or to self-insure. More often than not, people feel that long-term-care premiums are cost prohibitive. This leads them to take the self-insuring path. Please understand that the uncertainty associated with long-term-care costs can very plausibly result in all of your assets being depleted.

Ask yourself if you are honestly at peace with a situation that can end up leaving nothing to your kids, grandkids, or charities. We have found that, when pressed, most people are not OK with that outcome.

The next question you need to ask is "What is the minimum amount of money I want to leave behind in the worst-case scenario?" Whatever that amount happens to be, you need to then purchase either a linked-benefit policy or a traditional life-insurance policy to cover this need. This method certainly isn't free.

If you compare the life-insurance premium where you are certain to have value with the expense of a long-term-care premium that you might never use, you may find a higher level of comfort with choosing to self-insure your long-term-care risk. Even if you only leverage for a portion of your risk, you are at least retaining some control over your future.

Some points to consider would be these:

- Do you have relatives nearby that are able and willing to help provide care?

- What assets can be set aside or leveraged for the possibility of a long-term-care need?
- Does your company provide a long-term-care policy as part of its benefits package?
- Do you need to insure the whole amount, or will you be comfortable with minimum coverage?
- Will you be leaving anyone behind in a poor financial situation if you don't have long-term-care insurance?
- If you buy a traditional policy, can you afford an increase in premiums of 5 to 15 percent a year?

The big challenge is that long-term-care insurance is complex on every level. You must decide if you need it and when the best time is to start looking at options. When you look at the options, does it make more sense to use a traditional policy or a linked-benefit policy? Should you go with full coverage or just hedge your bets? Do you need an inflation rider or not? Should you combine it with a spouse's policy or a stand-alone? What is the true cost of self-insuring?

Those questions require a detailed look at your specific situation and personal attitudes. This will require you to talk to a specialist in the area of long-term care. Good financial coaches will bring this area up, but don't be surprised if they refer you to someone on their team or a colleague to make sure you get the best guidance possible.

We will leave this subject with a quote from Alan McLellan, the esteemed adjunct professor of insurance at the American College. Alan cleverly explains that "another compelling reason to have long-term-care insurance is that you might have an uncle who likes to brag that he goes to the bathroom every day at 7:00 a.m. But who unfortunately doesn't get out of bed until 8:00 a.m."

Summary

On that lighter note, it is easy to buy the wrong type of insurance much like it is easy to buy cheap beer. The difference is that when you buy the wrong beverage, it is easier and less expensive to correct the mistake.

When you purchase the wrong form of insurance, it can end up seriously hurting you financially. The hurt rarely comes right away.

Instead, it usually happens years later, and the cost can be quite significant. If you discover the error when you are still young, it is possible to recover. At some point, it might become impossible to correct the mistake. You don't want to arrive at retirement and realize you still have a need for insurance. You could easily be faced with significantly higher costs to "Protect It," or worse yet, you might find that you are no longer insurable. Therefore, it is essential to work with a financial coach to help you plan for your insurance needs of today and tomorrow.

CHAPTER 4

TAKE IT

*The question isn't at what age I want
to retire, it's at what income.*
—GEORGE FOREMAN, FORMER PROFESSIONAL
BOXER AND HEAVYWEIGHT CHAMPION

Take a moment and think back to what we mentioned in the "Plan It" chapter about what you are planning on doing this coming weekend. It may include spending time with family or working on a hobby. Maybe you will be taking some needed personal time to relax with a great book or movie. Quite possibly you are meeting with good friends.

Now stop and ask yourself how many Saturdays you have left. That's an odd question. But really, how many Saturdays will you have in retirement? A person retiring at age sixty-five and living to life expectancy only has about one thousand of them. What do you want to do on those Saturdays? Who do you want to spend them with, and where do you want to be? Retirement is nothing if not a week of Saturdays.

Few of us think of retirement this way, but we probably should because it personalizes the abstract concept of retirement planning. For most people, the destination of being retired may seem like such a long way off. The truth is that it will arrive quicker than you think, and many of the decisions you make today will directly impact all those answers about your future Saturdays.

When it comes to all those future Saturdays, you are going to care about both their quantity and quality. If you're struggling with an illness near the end of your life, then that puts an even higher premium on those earlier Saturdays in retirement. You will want to ensure you stay in control of as many as you can.

When someone asks you when you want to retire, your mind immediately goes to the age you will stop working. For most people, we start around age sixty-five and move up or down from there. That is because we have been programmed. We think sixty-five because that is when Social Security was originally set to begin, and it is still when Medicare becomes available.

Add to that the fact that we are an age-based society. As you grow up, you usually have a pretty good idea of the ages at which you will graduate, get a job, get married, have kids, send your kids to college, and, as we said, plan to retire. The funny thing is that Mr. Foreman is so right, and how most people plan is so wrong. You should not be evaluating when you want to retire in terms of age; instead you need to know how much income it will take to maintain your lifestyle. In other words, you can retire when you want, but when you retire dictates how much income you can expect to receive during your golden years.

When retirees and preretirees are asked, "What is your biggest concern?" running out of money continues to be at the top of the list.[1] It should be the biggest concern since for most people it is the largest risk. That is why no other section of this entire book matters more if you get it wrong.

To state it another way, you cannot screw up how you take money when you retire because it is almost impossible to fix if you do. If you are not careful, you will wipe out thirty to forty effective years of "Grow It" and end up eighty-five, broke, and living off just Social Security. The issue is that there are several risks, challenges, and complexities that make it difficult to get that dollar amount right. That is why it is so important to have help when you plan to "Take It."

If you look back at the last hundred years in the United States, you will see that taking income through retirement has never been more challenging than it is today. When your parents and grandparents retired with Social Security and a pension from work, they could maintain a reasonable lifestyle. Interest rates were notably higher while life expectancies were shorter.

As we are sure you are aware, that is no longer the case. Along with the emotional pitfalls, these economic challenges make planning essential. The key to making your personal finances last as long as you do is controlling your money and emotions. A common error is that retirees mistakenly allow the stock market, interest rates, and the economy to dictate their retirement-income stability instead of things they can control.

When it comes to taking money in retirement, there are three emotional landmines. The first one is getting too conservative too quickly. This happens when people worry their accounts could go down to zero, and they feel it would be disastrous to lose even a penny. This emotional concern arises out of a misunderstanding that you don't need much growth in retirement.

Also, anytime the market has a large loss, which gets hyped up by the media, this emotional misbehavior is reinforced. The Chicken Littles of the world run around yelling that the sky is falling. People respond by moving their money into more conservative investments at the worst possible times, which translates into lower return potential. During your working years, the trade-off for a lower return on your money is that you must save more. In retirement, that switches over to living off less income, which may not even be an option.

The second emotional response to watch out for is attempting to make money by getting too aggressive too late. We have had several conversations with people who tell us that they are more on the conservative side when it comes to investing, but when we look at where their money is, they are aggressively positioned. It can be very unnerving to be a few years from retiring and realize that you don't have enough saved.

Regrettably, one way people deal with this shortfall is by convincing themselves that if they just get a better return between now and retirement, it will make up the deficit. Using the markets to catch up is a recipe to experience a major market downturn at a critical time. We believe you should have part of your money invested for twenty to thirty years down the road. Just be sure to not keep your money that you need for income purposes invested too aggressively.

The third behavioral landmine to avoid is thinking that you can take income the same way your parents or grandparents did. The financial world they lived in no longer exists. Low interest rates, longer life expectancy, medical breakthroughs, increased market volatility, and an avalanche of information with no context have put us all in a position that means we must forge a different path.

Ultimately, this new reality is a good thing. Retirees today have more options and flexibility than ever before to create more meaningful retirements than any preceding generation.

A Closer Look at the Challenges

Here is the great news—as Americans, we are living longer. The bad news is also that we are living longer. Increased longevity creates the first major challenge when it comes to income planning. It is vital to make sure your money doesn't run out before you do. If you know exactly when you will pass away, this is not as much of a challenge.

Take your money, divide by the years you have left, and boom, you are done. Unfortunately, none of us knows how long we will live; we can promise you, though, that it is most likely longer than you think. To get an idea for how long you might live, you can go to www.living-to100.com and answer the questions. Based on your lifestyle and family history, the website will provide a life-expectancy age. That will provide you with a better idea of how long you will live. For some of you, this means that you might have to plan on being around into your nineties or even later.

We will add a twist to make it more of a challenge. If you are married, you need to account for not one, but two lives. As you can see in the chart below, for a married couple, there is a 25 percent chance of one of them living to or past age ninety-seven. That can significantly stretch out how long you will need your retirement income to last.

How long will you live?

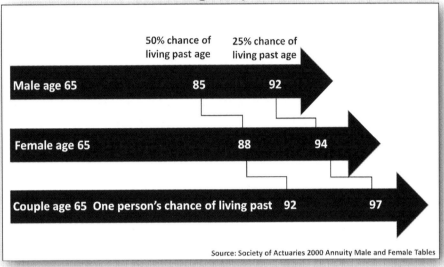

Source: Society of Actuaries 2000 Annuity Male and Female Tables

In 1980, you could get a CD that paid 17.74 percent. In 2015, the average six-month rate was 0.85 percent.[2] This interest-rate environment has forced people to move from more secure tools such as CDs into other options that may create more volatility, excessive risk, or less liquidity.

The old approach of living off the interest from FDIC-backed accounts is long gone and unlikely to return. Overall, what this means is that you may have to place more money in bonds to get enough interest income. That ties right back into being too conservative with your assets.

In the "Grow It" chapter, we talked about leveraging DCA while the markets go up and down. When you are investing, this is a great strategy because the dips in the market price provide buying opportunities. However, when you need to pull money out for income on a monthly or annual basis, that same volatility can mean you deplete your account too quickly.

Many experts state that 4 percent is the recommended withdrawal rate. A 4 percent withdrawal rate will statistically provide you with a 90 percent chance of not running out of money over thirty years. This means that on $1 million of investments, you can withdraw $40,000 a year.

Now let's make a wild suggestion that the markets lose 10 percent one year, and your million is now worth $900,000. What does that mean for your next year's income? Well, 4 percent of the lower number is $36,000. Your income is reduced by 10 percent, but your needs probably didn't decrease, meaning the percentage being drawn down increases to 4.4 percent if you pull out the same $40,000. If you don't reduce your income, then you have now increased your odds of running out of money too soon.

Withdrawal Rate Risk

Stock/Bond Mix	100/0	80/20	60/40	40/60	20/80
How withdrawal rate and portfolio allocation impact odds of success					
3% Withdrawal Rate	91%	97%	98%	98%	98%
4% Withdrawal Rate	82%	85%	90%	89%	83%
5% Withdrawal Rate	72%	78%	78%	71%	56%

Based on 30 years and adjusted for inflation.
Source: Wade Pfau http://www.fa-mag.com/news/new-research-challenges-4-withdrawal-rule-8674.html

When you consistently pull money out of the market, it is called taking systematic withdrawals. Quite literally, taking systematic withdrawals is the same thing as reverse dollar-cost averaging. In the example above, where you originally needed $40,000 annually, you sold however many shares were necessary to generate that income level.

But with the 10 percent market decline, your shares are now worth less in year two. Therefore, you have to sell more shares to generate that same $40,000 of income. You can see how this scenario could gut your portfolio prematurely.

The converse is also true. If you saw a 10 percent rise in your account balance, your shares would be worth more, and then you would get the benefit of needing to redeem fewer shares in year two to generate that same $40,000 you need.

The way to summarize reverse DCA is to say that the higher the market goes, the less you sell, and the lower the market goes, the more you sell. Wait, isn't that backward? We thought the way to make money is by buying low and selling high. Of course it is! Don't adopt an income strategy where you are doing the exact opposite of what you know represents the right way to make money.

Another challenge is that once you sell a share, whether high or low, you forfeit any future earnings potential on that share. This creates sequence-of-returns and withdrawal-rate risks. You cannot control what price a share will be on any given day. All you can control is whether you buy, sell, or hold on to it.

If you look at the charts below, you can see how this plays out in retirement. When you are not in control of when or how much you sell because you need the money, things can get nasty.

One of the major rule changes between growing your money and taking your money as income is that average annual rates of return no longer matter. The sequence of the returns risk is where your focus should be. It has a direct impact on the magnitude of risk from taking too high of a withdrawal rate.

Sequence of Returns

Year	1	2	3	4	5	6	7	8	9	10	11	12	13	14	15	16	17	18	19	20	Avg
Market Down Early	-15	-5	-15	5	25	20	10	15	5	10	15	10	20	0	5	10	5	15	10	15	8%
Market Down Late	10	25	15	5	10	10	25	15	5	15	10	20	10	5	0	15	5	-15	-5	-15	8%
Steady Growth	8	8	8	8	8	8	8	8	8	8	8	8	8	8	8	8	8	8	8	8	8%

All three scenarios have the same average rate of return of 8% starting with $500,000. When you take income at a 5% drawdown the ending values are:

- Market Down Early is around $150,000.
- Market Down Late is a little above $1,000,000.
- Steady Growth is about $350,000.

As we discussed earlier, inflation is another income-planning reality that cannot be ignored. The easiest way to describe inflation is to simply say that during your golden years, all the things you need to buy will cost more every year. The result will likely be an erosion of a substantial portion of your purchasing power. Your cash flow will buy you less and less over a thirty-year period. For example, at 3 percent, the value of your dollar in twenty years is cut to $0.55, and to $0.41 in thirty years.

Your assets must generate income and at the same time keep pace with inflation. That is a significant challenge since you most likely will not have alternative avenues to generate income when you are eighty-five years old—unless, of course, your retirement dream was to be a door greeter at a discount store.

We just mentioned the effects of a 3 percent inflation rate. Was that the correct rate to quote? We ask because a very sensitive topic for senior citizens is health care. Do you think health care will be less expensive or more expensive when you retire?

The cost of health care increased at a 5.1 percent rate from August 2015 to 2016. This is right around where it has tracked for the past decade.[3] As the US population continues to age, the demands for health-care resources will increase. It is fantastic that technology keeps people alive longer, but the costs are becoming excessive enough that they potentially need to be planned for years in advance. You may be able to reduce certain expenses, but that gap will be at least partially exacerbated by increased medical costs.

Generating Income

Traditionally, when most people retire, they take all the money they have worked hard to save over the years and throw it figuratively into a big pile.

Once people retire, they expect the money to do three things at the same time for them: First, they try to never lose any money. Second, they try to make as much money as they can. Third, they try to take income.

In your head right now, we want you to imagine a three-person tug-of-war with all three participants pulling in opposite directions. Money-management strategies for capital preservation, capital appreciation, and income distribution have very little in common. What happens is that people end up not doing any of the three strategies well.

One problem with this tactic is that, without realizing what they are doing, people effectively end up taking their entire portfolio and turning it into an emergency fund. Another huge problem with this approach is that those people are not in control. The market, dividends, interest rates, and unexpected events in a person's life are in control.

You have to change when those factors change. The last place you want to be in retirement is hoping the markets go up 12 percent, so you don't have to reenter the workforce. When you do it the traditional way, that is exactly what you are setting yourself up for at some point. You need a better strategy if you want to enjoy retirement. Staying in control is much more enjoyable.

Think about everything we told you about the right approach and behavior in the "Grow It" chapter. Now toss it out the window for this chapter. The rules of how you grow money do not apply when you begin taking income.

At the beginning of the movie *The Matrix*, the main character, Neo, sees the projection of the matrix, the world as he's being manipulated into seeing it. At the end of the movie, the walls and people disappear and are replaced with the green ones and zeroes that make up "the code." At that point, Neo sees the matrix as it really exists. Once he understands how it truly works, he gains the ability to control his own fate.

You have to be able to view taking money in retirement with the same clarity with which Neo can see the code. In the world of income distribution, the code is the payout rate. This is the only thing that really matters and is the only way to fairly evaluate each form of income distribution.

Payout rate is essentially the percentage of how much you can expect to receive in income from your assets. Each method to increase your payout will have trade-offs. When you know the trade-offs, then you can evaluate which one makes the most sense for you.

To determine how much payout you need, start with how much it will cost you to live in retirement. We would love to admit that what we are about to say is not groundbreaking, but based on what we see people actually doing and what many advisors still recommend, it just might be.

When you start planning your income in retirement, you have to break it into two categories: what you must have and what you would like to have. "Must have" includes basic food, clothing, and shelter. The "want to have" category is all the rest. This can be a little blurry for some people.

You need to eat, but do you need to eat steak every night? You need a car, but do you need a Lexus? We get it that everyone wants to believe that the Lexus is a must, but it isn't. You are in control of deciding what it is that you can't live without and set that as your baseline.

You will need to break down your expenses this way, so you know how much you plan to spend during your thirty-year retirement. How much is "must have," and how much is "want to have"? Whatever falls in the "must have" category needs to be fully covered as long as you are breathing.

There are three ways to safely guarantee enough income for life that will cover your "must haves"—Social Security, pensions, and lifetime income annuities. You can always cover more of your income needs with these guaranteed sources. That makes sense if you are risk averse or if you may not be able to curb your emotional behaviors after you retire. To help you determine which ones make sense, we will review each of these guaranteed income streams so you understand how they work and how best to leverage them to ensure that you to stay in control.

Social Security

Let's play a quick game of "How Much Do You Want?" It is super easy. There is no right or wrong answer. We will list some different dollar figures that you can take as a lump sum value at retirement, assuming you will live to age eight-five.

Option One: $574,015 at sixty-two
Option Two: $608,110 at sixty-seven
Option Three: $610,458 at seventy

Which one do you choose and why?

OK, round two. You will still have three options, but now they are going to be listed as monthly incomes.

Option One: $1,658 at sixty-two
Option Two: $2,367 at sixty-seven
Option Three: $2,941 at seventy

That's it. There is no bonus round. This dollar figure is what you get to choose from as income for the rest of your life. Which one did you choose and why?

Again, there's no right or wrong answer, but did you pick the same age in both options? If not, welcome to the interesting trait of how we comprehend money in payments versus lump-sum values over time.

The choices are the same, just looked at from different angles. Option One is the lifetime value of Social Security at sixty-two, Option Two is at full retirement of sixty-seven, and Option Three is delaying to the maximum payment at age seventy. Interestingly, most people opt for age sixty-two when they look at the monthly income, but that flips when it is shown as a lump sum. Most people decide to delay to full retirement or later when they see the large value.

Why? Psychology is the culprit. When looking at the difference between the monthly amounts, most people make certain assumptions that influence their choices. The first assumption is that they are not giving up too much by starting early, and since they start early, they will get more over their lifetimes.

Also, they do not consider that, historically, Social Security has had an inflation increase most years. It may not be much, but over fifteen, twenty, or thirty years, it makes a significant difference. By the way, that inflation increase is calculated from your starting paycheck. The higher the first paycheck, the more that 1 percent to 2 percent cost-of-living adjustment turns out to be.

The other assumption is that you must get it while the getting is good. Not surprisingly, people do not trust the federal government to fulfill its promise, so they go with a "bird in the hand versus two in the bush" philosophy and take it early. This is another great example of getting too conservative too quickly.

Waiting a few years to take basically no risk to have your payment grow by at least 8 percent each year is a good bet. Taking it early because it feels better is an overly conservative choice. It is easier to see how much you give up in the lump-sum choice; hence the shift.

So that brings us to when you should take Social Security. Unless you have a very compelling reason to take it early, our advice is to take it later. Use other money that does not grow at an 8 percent rate each year instead.

When you look at all the data, which we will not bore you with, rarely does it makes sense for the primary wage earner to opt in at sixty-two.

If you are married, the purpose of delaying the primary wage earner to age seventy is that when the first spouse dies, the remaining spouse takes over or continues the higher of the two monthly checks. In other words, the higher earner's Social Security check becomes a joint and survivor lifetime annuity. If you want a paycheck to last two lives, we can tell you that you need it to be the highest check possible.

In certain situations, it does make sense to take Social Security at sixty-two. If you look at your life expectancy and realize there is little chance of getting to age eighty-two due to illness or family history, or you do not have a spouse dependent on your check at some point, then taking it early could work out. If you are the lower-earning spouse, then it could be better to start early. You might be taking over the higher paycheck, so get the money earlier. What we will tell you, though, is that delaying your start pays off the clear majority of the time.

Pensions

Once upon a time, pensions covered the retirement landscape. A person would work hard and stay with the same company. The reward for this loyalty was that at retirement, he or she was handed a gold watch and a pension. The pension was a stream of income that lasted for his or her whole life and sometimes that of the spouse. In 2011 around 18 percent of the private workforce still had a pension as part of their retirement plan.[4]

The lucky few that still have a pension plan are often provided the choice at retirement to either take a lump sum or a lifetime payment option. They can be paid solely for their lifetimes or add a survivor benefit of usually 50 percent to 100 percent of the first payee's income. If you choose this option, the payment will be decreased accordingly for the increased time the pension will have to pay.

If you happen to be one of the few with a pension coming to you at retirement, you most likely have a couple of questions. The biggest of these is whether to take the pension as a lifetime stream of income or as a lump sum. There is a mathematical answer. This is where you look at how much you are going to get paid over how long you think you will live. Then compare that to the lump sum earning a rate of return stretched out over the same time. If you look at the chart below, it will show you how it works in two different scenarios.

Pension Decision

Lump Sum Payout vs. Monthly Income Payout

Male age 65
Option 1: $200k Lump Sum
Option 2: $1,200 monthly income for life
Option 3: $1,000 monthly income with 75% Survivor Female age 65

Option 1 vs. Option 2		Option 1 vs. Option 3	
Rate of Return	Years it Will Last	Rate of Return	Years it Will Last
3%	17	3%	23
4%	20	4%	27
5%	23	5%	35
6%	29	6%	88

There is also an emotional answer that, much of the time, goes for the income payment. Thankfully, there is no need to do math on this choice. What may be surprising is that we will tell you to be more emotional on this decision. There are three reasons, from our perspective.

The first is that, as we have said before, it puts you in better emotional control, knowing you will never run out of money. The second reason is that if you have your "must haves" covered, then it will allow your other assets to continue to grow over time. Third, you probably will live longer than the pension plan expects, meaning you will get more money over time with zero chance of running out.

Lifetime Income Annuity

So, when you sit down and calculate what you will need as an income floor, the likelihood is low that Social Security and pension payments will cover all of it. If they don't, then you may have to make up the gap using one of your other assets to purchase a lifetime income annuity.

Think of a lifetime income annuity as buying your own pension plan from an insurance company. You pay a premium, and based on the amount you pay, current interest-rate assumptions, life expectancy, and gender, the insurance company will pay you a set amount of income for the rest of your life. Like a pension, this can provide income for two people's lives with optional guarantees to make sure income lasts if you die prematurely. The older you are and the higher the current interest rates, the higher your payout rate will be.

You can see below that the payout as you get older creates leverage that surpasses what you can get in many other financial tools.

Lifetime Income Annuity Payouts

Age	Male	Female	Joint
60	5.4%	5.3%	5.0%
65	5.9%	5.7%	5.4%
70	6.6%	6.3%	6.0%
75	7.5%	7.1%	6.7%
80	8.6%	8.1%	7.8%
85	10.0%	9.4%	9.1%

Illustrated in state of CO on $100,000 using Life with cash refund option 12/2016
Source: https://www.immediateannuities.com/

We mentioned there are trade-offs. If you are being provided income for the rest of your life with no risk, what do you have to give up? The first thing is access to your money. Some companies do provide limited access to a portion of your original purchase price, but they have hedged the deal to their favor, so assume you have zero liquidity. Therefore, you should never put all your money here.

The next item is growth. Just like Social Security or pensions, you get what you get, and you don't throw a fit. Over many years, as we have said, inflation will creep up, and the value of the check will be diminished. You can add an option to have your payment increase at a set percent each year, but if you plan properly, you will not need it.

There are two ways to hedge the reality of inflation. The first is to have enough in investable assets to help offset the decrease in purchasing power. The second option is to set aside some assets that will begin paying you later. A deferred-income annuity might make sense in this scenario. It works just like it sounds.

You put money in as a lump sum or a series of payments with the idea that income will start when you are older. The longer you wait, the higher the payment will be. When it starts, it will increase your current income and hopefully offset any increase of living costs.

Lack of liquidity and growth are fair criticisms of income annuities. However, another way to look at the issue of inflation is to always remember that it affects all income the same. It doesn't matter the income source. Regardless, 3 percent inflation is 3 percent inflation.

Keeping that in mind, could an income annuity help fight inflation's effects? As mentioned earlier, we believe you need to keep an appropriate amount of money invested in the stock market to outpace inflation. Remember those investor-behavior statistics from "Grow It?" They weren't good.

Start thinking now about a vision for your retirement. Recall that this income-annuity check is completely guaranteed. Interest rates won't make it go down, and a stock-market drop won't either. If the market drops but your income remains exactly the same, you will feel less pressure to place a panicked sell order in your portfolio at the wrong time. Having your income guaranteed will counterintuitively help you outpace inflation with your equity investments because you will be an investor-behavior superstar.

The second option is an idea from the federal government that doesn't completely suck. One of the issues you will face if you have done everything right is the required minimum distribution (RMD) rule. Basically, what this rule says is that the year after you turn seventy and one-half, you must start taking a certain portion out of your traditional

IRAs. Each year as you get older, the required amount increases as a percentage of your account balance.

To help create more income security for retirees, the government created qualified longevity annuity contracts (QLAC). These are deferred-income annuities that allow you to place Traditional IRA money into them and avoid the RMD on that portion by deferring the first payment until as late as age eighty-five. This helps reduce unnecessary taxes as well as guarantee income for life. You can add your spouse and a second payee as well. If you do happen to pass away, any unpaid amount will go to your beneficiary.

It is necessary to note that you will be depending on an insurance company to provide income for a long time. Therefore, you must review the ratings and financial stability of the company. As we advised in the "Protect It" chapter, do not use a company that is rated less than an A- by the rating agencies or has a Comdex under 85. You are depending on this paycheck for the rest of your life; make sure the insurance company will be there to fulfill its obligation.

In the book *SuperFreakonomics*, authors Steven D. Levitt and Steven J. Dubner have a great conversation about how some people live longer than others. One of the methods to extend your time on earth is to buy an annuity because the "steady payout provides a little extra incentive to keep chugging along."

We completely agree with them, but we would also point out that if you know you will never run out of income, you are much less stressed than the other way around. Between Social Security, a pension, and an income annuity, you will be more content because you will have more control with fewer worries.[5] That sounds like a more enjoyable way to be retired.

Once you have covered your basic income needs with sources of guaranteed income that last for the rest of your life, you are done. Well, not really, but you have reduced and maybe even removed that three-way tug-of-war. With an income floor, you will have more freedom to decide how to handle your other assets.

It is important to remember that we have now reduced the systematic-withdrawal and withdrawal-rate risks because all the income needs from the asset will be "wants." We know you do not want to put off buying the new boat, but if your investments are down, the cost of that boat will be more than what is shown on the price tag.

Other Assets

Once you have your worst-case income scenario established from the guidance above, you can now turn to how best to handle your remaining assets. There are a few options, and we will outline each, but again, this is where a financial coach comes into play. He or she will know which one will provide the best leverage within any given economic and personality situation.

The key is these assets need to be able to offset inflation over time as well as provide access for unforeseen or uninsured risks. Do not, under any situation, get too conservative. If you have used an income annuity, the proper mind-set to have is that it represents a portion of your bond allocation.

Think of it this way: If you are supposed to have 40 percent of your money in bonds, and the amount you placed in the income annuity equals 15 percent of your investable assets, you only need to place another 25 percent into actual bond holdings. If you get too conservative too soon, you will find that in twenty to thirty years, you have problems that could have been avoided.

Shifting to Payout Rate

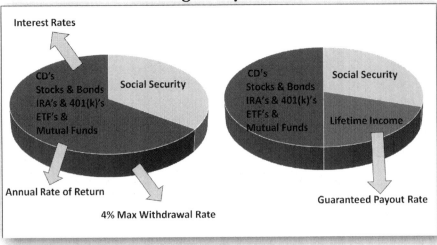

Let's start off with the 4 percent withdrawal. The 4 percent can come only from your stock positions, or you can include your bonds as well. This now becomes easier because you have the choice to reduce it each year or not take it at all. You are back in control.

If you do not include your bonds within the 4 percent, a great strategy is to set it up to take the dividends. We advise to take about 75 percent of the dividends produced and let the remaining 25 percent reinvest to purchase additional shares.

Over time you will be increasing how much you receive in dividends as you add more shares to your portfolio. The chart below walks through what this looks like over ten years.

Hypothetical $100,000 in Bond Fund

Year	Share Price at NAV	Annual Dividend	75% of Dividend Taken as Income	Shares Purchased	Total Shares
1/3/2017	$5.69			17,574	17,574
12/2017	$5.72	$6,116	$4,587	267	17,841
12/2018	$5.74	$6,209	$4,657	270	18,111
12/2019	$5.75	$6,303	$4,727	274	18,385
12/2020	$5.64	$6,398	$4,799	281	18,666
12/2021	$6.10	$6,496	$4,872	266	18,932
12/2022	$7.33	$6,588	$4,941	225	19,157
12/2023	$7.50	$6,667	$5,000	222	19,379
12/2024	$6.62	$6,744	$5,058	255	19,634
12/2025	$5.51	$6,832	$5,124	310	19,944
12/2026	$5.69	$6,941	$5,205	305	20,249
			Total Income: $48,970		Ending Value: $115,217

Assumes steady dividend of $0.0297 a share paid out monthly and all reinvested at year end.

Lastly, there is the common bucket approach. With this strategy, you will build three buckets of money. The initial bucket is money you will take as "want" income for the next five to ten years. An intermediate bucket will be midrange money to replace the first bucket. Finally, you'll have a third bucket for growth. The idea is that if you use money with an intention, it works more efficiently.

Now, Later, Much Later, and Never

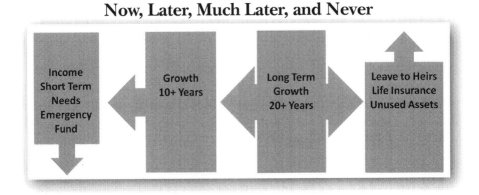

So, which strategy should you choose? Hopefully by now you already know that answer—the one you feel most comfortable with.

Guaranteed Withdrawal

Here is a twist on the above to consider. Imagine being able to invest your money for growth and get a guarantee that you can take a set percentage out each year without ever running out of money. Does it sound too good to be true? Well, it is, and it isn't.

This goes back to when we talked about extra parachutes in "Grow It." How it works is an insurance company uses a variable or index annuity that allows investment values to be locked in at account peaks known as high-water marks and many times at a guaranteed growth rate of, say, 5 percent. These guaranteed values provide a benefit base value from which to draw income. This benefit base does not decrease if you follow the contract rules regarding withdrawal amounts and investment options.

When the time comes for income, the owner can withdraw up to a certain percentage of the benefit value based on the contract provisions. This withdrawal can be stopped and started. If the actual account value goes all the way down to zero, the withdrawal can continue until death even though you are technically out of real money. That is the good part.

As radio legend Paul Harvey used to say, "And now, the rest of the story." You will be paying for the cost of insurance. Many of these riders are well over 1 percent a year in cost, and due to limited investment options inside the variable annuity, you may not be able to invest aggressively enough to justify the additional expense.

Here is the kicker; to get the most value out of the rider, the best approach is to start taking the money within ten years and never stop, even if you do not need the income. Think of it this way: If you can take 6 percent of your benefit as income each year, it will take you nearly seventeen years to draw out your guaranteed value. You come out ahead every year after seventeen years, so start it and take it to make sure you are beating the insurance company.

Reverse Mortgages

For most people, their greatest asset when they hit retirement is not their 401(k) account. Rather, it is the home in which they live. Until recently there was never an economical way to access that value without selling the home. Let's be honest; you still need to live somewhere, so selling your home may not be much of an option. Even with the previous guaranteed-income advice, some people may still be worried about running out of money.

We get it since we also know that life never, and we mean *never*, works out like you think it should. That is why we know it is best to always have a hedge. The ace up your sleeve for money in retirement is a reverse mortgage, formally known as a home equity conversion mortgage, or HECM. Up until the early part of this decade, these were not a great option for many reasons.

In 2012 the federal government made some legislative changes that make these not only better, but often an essential part of many retirement plans. In fact, Wade Pfau, professor of Retirement Income at the American College and director of Retirement Research at McLean Asset Management and inStream Solutions, stated that a reverse mortgage "strategically can help improve clients' retirement sustainability and build a larger legacy to leave their heirs."[6] In plain English, this means you could be better off with one than without one.

How you get the money out of the reverse mortgage is also more flexible than in the past. The traditional way is that you take the reverse mortgage as a stream of income that lasts for a lifetime. That is not a bad option, but for anyone that might think they will need the leverage for income, medical costs, or modifications to their home to adapt it to older living, you can set up the reverse mortgage and not use it right away.

We will say that again, you can sign up for a reverse mortgage and never use it, but it is on tap and ready to go in case you do. If you do leave it for later, your account will earn interest that will beat what you are getting in safe money today. Since we know most people are retiring with less-than-optimal funds, this becomes a no-brainer.

When you leave the house, whatever is owed to the reverse-mortgage company is taken out of the sale price. As an example, if you owe $150,000 and the house is sold for $200,000, your beneficiaries will get $50,000, and the rest goes to the reverse mortgage company. If you owe the same $150,000 and the house sells for $140,000, the mortgage company is responsible for the loss.

When does a reverse mortgage not make any sense? If you want to leave the home to someone specific, he or she would have to buy out the mortgage company for what is owed to keep the property. Also, if you plan to downsize later, be aware of what options are available to you when considering the reverse mortgage.

When a reverse mortgage is used along with the other strategies above, you decrease the odds of running out of money in your retirement. Consider it as an insurance policy for your golden years.

Taxes

We are sure you are aware of the saying that the only things certain in life are death and taxes. When it comes to taxes, we are also certain that we have no idea what they will be when you retire. Conventional wisdom has been that when you retire, you will be in a lower tax bracket. This is based off the idea that you will have less income and lower expenses in retirement than during your working years.

It is true that you most likely will not be contributing to retirement accounts (3 to 20 percent of income), nor will you will be paying FICA (7.65 to 15.3 percent on the first $118,000). If nothing changes, you are good. Now stop for a second and ask yourself this question: "Do you think that tax brackets will be lower, the same, or higher in the future?"

How you answer that determines how you will plan for efficient tax maneuvering when you retire. A great way to minimize taxes is to use Betterment LLC's tax strategy, which we'll discuss later in the "Choose It" chapter. A good coach will make sure you have money in accounts with a variety of tax treatment to help you maximize tax-location strategies.

Let's turn to a quick primer on how the progressive tax structure works in the good old United States. There are currently seven different brackets, and that will probably change a couple of times during your lifetime. Most people hear that they are in a tax bracket and assume that means all the money they earned was paid at that rate.

The first bracket of 10 percent hits the first chunk of your income, the next chunk is at 15 percent, and so on all the way to the top. When you get to the highest level of your income, that is what most people identify as their bracket. Since each chunk was charged at its own rate, you end up with a blended rate.

The easy rule of thumb is to subtract eight from the top tier (28 percent minus 8 percent = 20 percent), and that is close to what your effective tax rate on all your income will be. Obviously, this can vary, but it gives you the idea. This is important because when you are done working, have paid off the mortgage (hopefully), and the kids are all gone, so are all the tax deductions you were receiving. Now you must navigate controlling taxes. The more you prepare during your "Grow It" years, the easier that will be for you.

How money is treated taxwise comes down to if it is fully taxable, sort of taxable, or not taxable at all. Traditional IRAs, 401(k)s, pensions, SEPs, SIMPLEs, 403(b)s, and the like are tax deferred while they grow but then fall in the fully taxable column upon withdrawal. Roth 401(k), Social Security, brokerage accounts, stocks, bonds, and IRAs with non-deducted portions go in the sort-of-taxable column. Roth IRAs, income from tax-free municipal bonds, health savings accounts (HSA) if used for qualified medical costs, and cash value life insurance (if accessed the proper way) hit the tax-free column.

Let's walk through a tax scenario in the chart below to see how having different tax accounts in retirement can have an impact. We will assume a married couple with an annual income need of $100,000.

Tax Diversification

	Fully Taxable	Taxable and Tax Free
401(k)	$85,000	$50,000
Traditional IRA's	$15,000	$15,000
Roth IRA	$0	$25,000
HSA	$0	$10,000
Cash Flow	$100,000	$100,000
Taxable Income	$100,000	$65,000
Less Exemptions	($8,100)	($8,100)
Less Standard Deductions	($12,600)	($12,600)
Taxable Income	$79,300	$44,300
Tax Bracket	25%	15%
Tax Due	$11,368	$5,718

That is the power of picking your own tax bracket. Not only does this couple pay less in taxes, more importantly, the extra savings can continue to grow and be there if needed.

One last item to consider is if you want to leave anything behind. This can change the order discussed above depending on how much you want to leave and to whom you want to leave it. We will cover this more in the next chapter, but for now just know that it may be better for you to pay taxes while you are alive than for your beneficiaries. If that is the case, then you would leave some or all the tax-free items behind to help reduce their tax burden.

Summary

The one part you cannot get wrong happens to be the hardest for people to do without help. It is essential to seek out a good coach that understands all the areas covered above. Don't do it just when you get ready to retire. Do it well before! We suggest working with a team since the process of you getting to and through retirement comfortably can span forty to sixty years. The likelihood of one coach being there that entire time is slim.

A few years ago, we had the opportunity to meet with a seventy-year-old widow. Her husband had passed away about a year earlier. As we learned more about her situation, it became clear that she had stopped spending money on anything but the bare essentials.

In fact, she mentioned that one of her greatest joys had been to take her grandkids to Pizza Hut every Saturday. Because of her fear of running out of money, now that her husband had passed away, she had even stopped doing these lunches.

Stop for a second. Do you think this is how she imagined her time as a grandmother in retirement? Ugh. Of course not! The truth is that you live your entire life with priorities that you pay for out of your paychecks. The priorities change when you retire, and even may be fewer, but they do not go away. At a minimum, you will still have taxes, groceries, utilities, car upkeep, Medicare, prescriptions, and home maintenance.

That, by the way, is not living; it is surviving. No one intentionally plans to merely survive retirement. So how could we help this lady? We showed her how to reposition some of her assets to have an income floor so that she knew no matter how long she lived, she could always afford to take the grandkids and great-grandkids to Pizza Hut like she intended.

She sent one of us a Christmas card later that year with a picture of her with her grandkids on one of their lunch outings. For the next eighty years, her grandchildren will remember her example of how to be a grandparent and then pass that tradition on in their families. It isn't always just about the money. She is definitely a success story we won't soon forget.

To complete this conversation, we will leave you with this question: "How much income do you need so you can spend your retirement years worry free?" It is OK if you can't answer that right now. A financial coach will be able to help answer that question as well as figure out the best method for your personality to take income. When your coach finds you the right income plan, go ahead and swipe right. Remember, you cannot be out of control and at peace.

CHAPTER 5
LEAVE IT

Plans are nothing; planning is everything.
—DWIGHT D. EISENHOWER

On the day you retire, every asset you own will end up either being spent or left behind. That's it. There is no in between, no gray area. Every dollar you have saved will either be "Take It" or "Leave It."

The only question is whether you have done the proper planning to make sure it happens the way you want. The truth is that you will most likely leave something behind. How much and in what way, though, is unclear unless you have proper planning in place. By not addressing this issue head on, many of us are creating unnecessary problems for our loved ones.

When the topic of estate planning comes up, most people think they don't need to worry about it because they don't have enough of anything, except maybe debt, to plan for an estate. The truth is that proper estate planning has little to do with how much money you do or don't have. Rather, it is about making sure that what you have goes to whom you want in the way you want. You spend your entire life trying to be in control of your money, so the last thing you should want to happen is that you have no control in the last stage.

Guess what—people are quite prone to mess this one up. Part of the challenge is that the period tends to be so far out there, but it also gets hit hard by our behaviors. There are many preconceived notions within this topic that can get us in trouble. To discuss the emotional pitfalls, we broke this section into three main categories: "Blind Eye Syndrome," "My Beneficiary Is What?" and "I Will Get to That Tomorrow."

Blind Eye Syndrome

Blind Eye Syndrome refers to all the things we don't and won't see. One major mental block is assuming everything will all work out. We should be very careful in the financial-services industry when using the word *guarantee*. In this case, we can use it, though. We *guarantee* that your estate plan will work itself out. It might be an utter disaster in the form of unnecessary taxes, damaged relationships, and unintended consequences. But it will work out, guaranteed.

Now, if you assume it will work out, *well,* then that is a different story. Many of us have the desire to do just about anything rather than spend the necessary time to enact effective planning. Closely tied in with this is avoidance. We tell ourselves it will work out fine, so we can avoid making the hard choices.

Nobody wants to admit hard things, like that an adult child drinks too much, gambles too much, is a drug addict, or can't keep a job. Sometimes children's issues aren't behavior related. Instead they involve complicated split families or huge differences in personal wealth or money-management disciplines. Any time there are personal or emotional issues involved, it just makes it easier to ignore the planning process when what you should be doing is coughing up the money to do it right.

Similar outcomes can occur for several reasons in the business world as well. A great example of this is partnerships. We have lost count of the businesses that say they have a succession or buyout plan in place when they have nothing outside of verbal agreements or vague ideas. This emotional and economic avoidance can create such havoc that getting even a basic plan in place should be at the top of the list.

Very few people want to be business partners with a deceased partner's spouse. Without proper planning and funding for a succession plan, that is exactly what can happen. If you avoid the issue and die, you don't care since you are dead. The bad news is that your still-living business partner and family get to deal with the mess you avoided. Or perhaps it would be better to say the mess you created.

Another blind eye we turn is with the "what if" scenarios. What if you get sick and need care? What if you get a divorce? What if you are sued? We ignore these because life always works out perfectly for everybody all the time, and by the way, we are immortal and imperishable. Wait, that last sentence isn't true at all. Yet, we live our lives like it is. We are not suggesting you go around being Debbie Downer, assuming everything will fall apart at every turn. We are saying that you need to have a plan with built-in flexibility in case something does not go as expected.

The final blind spot is when we think we can do estate planning all on our own. Certain companies feed into this with do-it-yourself (DIY) wills, trusts, buy-sell agreements, et cetera. You can do it yourself, but it is nearly impossible to do it right by yourself. Asking and paying for help are difficult emotional barriers to overcome. It can be argued that many things in life can be done on your own or at a better cost. Not here, though. Due to the complexities of estate and legacy planning, you will be better off with the right help.

The best approach is to assemble a team of experts. Depending on the complexity of your plan, you may only need a Certified Financial Planner ®, but most likely you will also need an estate-planning attorney, CPA, and insurance agent. Each one will bring different expertise to the table as well as a balancing factor to one another.

No one would field a baseball team with only six players on the field. Smart planning does not leave out aspects that must be done right. Imagine intending to leave a piece of property to a loved one. Instead of inheriting it, the intended recipient is forced to sell the property to pay for the tax settlement due to lack of liquidity. That is just one example of what can happen if you don't have the right advice.

My Beneficiary Is What?

Beneficiaries are unique because they deserve a thorough discussion from two different viewpoints: from the perspective of the person leaving a legacy and from the perspective of those inheriting the assets. Self-awareness is a struggle for many people. We all think we have a good grasp of who we are, yet when we start to get truthful feedback, we shy away from it. We, the authors, understand that sometimes the truth can be uncomfortable. When it comes to our beneficiaries, we don't always see them for who they really are.

We've dealt with clients in a multitude of situations when it comes to their heirs. As a case in point, there are twin brothers that were raised in an upper-middle-class family. How they were raised was similar, with no favoritism shown one way or another. Today, one of them is a very successful and responsible person. The other one is a professional mooch.

The mooch has never held down a job for more than a year, spends his time drinking and partaking of herbs, and soaks his dad for money whenever he gets in trouble. As annoying as this all happens to be, the responsible brother let it slide until his dad shared with him that he was ill and probably would pass away within the next year.

The dad wanted to get his estate in order. During the discussion, the responsible son pointed out that when his brother received his share of the sizeable inheritance, it would rapidly disappear. The responsible one feared that his brother would one day come knocking on his door the same way he had done to his father, looking for a handout. When confronted with this obvious fact, the dad's response was that he had not even considered it as a possibility.

Stop for a minute, and think about that. Anyone could easily see what a spendthrift the irresponsible son was, except the dad, who had been supporting his son's errant lifestyle for the last twenty-five years. Why did he not see the obvious?

The reason is he did not want to face the fact that his son, whom he raised properly, did not turn out to be a productive member of society. It was always much easier to make excuses than lay down the gauntlet and force him to improve. The frightening part is this story is true, and unfortunately, it is not an isolated one.

Some people are willing to open their eyes to see their beneficiaries for who they really are once it becomes necessary. Others choose to ignore the elephant in the room. We are reminded of a family with a child in severe financial trouble. He would take help up until it came to sitting down and putting together a budget. Everybody in the family knew the issue was a gambling addiction, but no one wanted to confront him. This elephant-in-the-room mentality can be extremely damaging to everyone involved. Having a financial coach and an expert team will provide the best opportunity to mitigate this planning hesitation.

Another aspect with regard to beneficiaries is how they deal with one another. Items that you own have emotional attachments for different people in different ways. We have seen siblings that were close throughout their lives cease talking to one another over a material item. Part of it is the grief that comes with losing a loved one, but part of it has to do with people believing that they will get something when a family member dies.

Yes, people—start thinking ahead as to what will happen when you die. Do not assume that everybody knows who should get what. You will be creating a problem that could impact lives for years to come. Make good use of a will to list every item you can think of. Also, talk to your heirs and ask if there is something they might want. You might be surprised as to what holds meaning for them.

It is essential to work with a financial coach who will take the time to meet and get to know each person who stands to receive part of your inheritance. They can play the role of determining how best to make sure the benefits are received, not only for your peace of mind, but for the best interest of each beneficiary. They will also ensure that everything is not only written down, but communicated to each of the beneficiaries so that there are no surprises during the grieving process.

Most importantly, they will not have emotional blinders on when it comes to the personalities involved. Please do not underestimate the magnitude of this section. As a parent, how you leave your assets to your beneficiaries is one of the very few decisions you will ever make that can either maintain or ruin your adult children's relationships after you are gone.

I Will Get to That Tomorrow!

"Never do today what can be put off until tomorrow." Welcome once again to the world of procrastination. As people, we always think that we have another day in our lives. How many times when we were kids did we hear "there's always tomorrow" after having a bad day? That belief makes it easy to convince ourselves we can take care of it tomorrow, so we put it off until tomorrow. Unfortunately, as the adage states, sometimes "tomorrow never comes."

Another way we procrastinate is to shy away from estate planning as a behemoth of a task. We look at everything that needs to be done, and we cringe at the amount of time, effort, and resources required. Doing anything else seems like it would be more appealing than planning for our ultimate demise.

Make It Happen

Let's face it; planning for when we die can be uncomfortable. Often people think it means that our goals and dreams have ended, all tied up neatly with the dismal black bow of a funeral. Wait. Hit the pause button. That is not at all what we are discussing here.

We are talking about everything that happens after that event. Stop for a moment, and consider what the most wonderful thing would be that you could do for your kids or grandkids. No limit except your imagination. So why don't you go do that right now?

Well, if you are like 99 percent of the world, you have restraints upon your life. You have bills and commitments. You need to make sure you make it through retirement comfortably. We get that. Since you do not have a specific expiration date, you need to hedge that a bit so you still have money if needed.

But now look at it from the other end. Imagine the gift you just thought of coming true after you pass away. The restraints are gone. Your heirs will remember that you not only cared about them when you were alive, but you cared enough to provide something lasting after you passed. That can only happen with a plan.

There are planners available for every aspect of your life, such as wedding planners, remodeling planners, academic planners, financial planners, and vacation planners. You might very well want to consider hiring a "Leave It" planner. If done properly, deciding what to leave should rightfully be a fun part of your planning. This is where you have an opportunity to change the future.

Cleaning House

Basic housecleaning is the simplest level of proper planning. This can be as basic as developing an accurate will and organizing files. Years ago, we sat across a lunch table with a coworker. She was explaining in brutal detail what had occupied the better part of her last three months. Her aunt had passed away, leaving all her possessions to some nieces and nephews.

Since our coworker was the aunt's favorite, the aunt named her in the will as the person to settle the matters of the remaining estate. It was great that there was a will, but it had not been updated for over ten years. Many of the named beneficiaries were deceased, couples were divorced, and new babies had been born.

Outside of the inaccurate will, the aunt had left very little in the way of instructions or organization. The niece had to go through every piece of paper to determine what was important as well as look for any accounts that might have been missed. After several months and repeated trips to banks and courts, as well as tough conversations with family members, she finalized her aunt's estate.

It's doubtful the aunt had any intention of creating a financial and emotional burden for her beloved niece, yet that is exactly what she did. The entire mess could have been avoided or greatly reduced with an updated will, some organized paperwork, and consolidated accounts.

A will may be all you need. If your children are minors, you can name their guardians in your will. You can also indicate your wishes for property and assets, along with other items. If you do not want the courts involved, though, you will need to take it to the next level, and that will require a trust. We will discuss that in more depth later.

Even with a will in place, there are still aspects of basic housecleaning that need to be handled. As we discussed in the last chapter, people are living longer. This is great in some ways, but approximately 50 percent of those age eighty and up struggle with some level of dementia. How do you stay in control when you are not aware that you are out of control?

This is when you need to make sure ahead of time that you have the appropriate powers of attorney in place. These documents provide a named person with the necessary legal authority to act on your behalf. If you make these documents durable, they last until they are revoked or you die. Many people make them "springing," so they only go into effect once an event happens.

You can also place limits as to what decisions they can make. You will want a medical power of attorney to allow someone else to make decisions regarding your health and treatment. For someone to help you handle money matters, you will want a financial power of attorney. Along these same lines, you will want a HIPPA authorization, so people can have access to your medical records. This way, you can stay in control even when you are not.

Conducting this complete housecleaning requires you to assimilate together a master copy of all your accounts, passwords, and contacts. Then you must place all the information in a safety deposit box or fire-proof safe. We know we are being Captain Obvious here, but don't forget where everything is kept, and let someone else know too. Otherwise all your hard work will be in vain.

We know of a woman that keeps copies of her powers of attorney with locations of important documents in her house, car, husband's car, and with each of her children. Might be a bit of overkill, but no matter what happens, someone will have the proper documents.

Many people hesitate to do even the most basic of planning because they are not 100 percent sure what they want to do. A word of wisdom— plans can always be changed, and it is far better to have part of your planning in place than none of it.

If you are a beneficiary, you will want to proactively start this process with your family members. If they are already working with a financial coach, accountant, or attorney, go with them to the next meeting. Build a relationship with all the advisors. You want to do this for two main reasons.

First, you need to know who you will be dealing with in the future. Second, you need to make sure the advice being provided is right. The specialist may not fully understand the family dynamics and personalities involved. You know how crazy your sister is and what will set her off. Mom, Dad, and the advisor may not.

Your insight can help head off issues farther down the road. Many so-called professionals will try to wing it so as not to give up a nice payday.

Make sure the advisor is actually qualified. It is better to find out now if the proper planning isn't being done, before it is too late.

Make It Last

For some people, the need for estate planning centers more on passing something of lasting value on to the following generations. There is a story of an extremely wealthy man who had several children. He worried that when he died, they would stop working, and his hard work would vanish due to luxurious lifestyles. Not wanting his wealth to dissipate this way, the man placed his money in a bank with trustees to oversee the money for the benefit of his children.

The catch was that the only way for anyone to receive any money, they had to come to the trustees with a business plan. If the plan was viable, the money would be lent out at a reasonable interest rate. The children were required to then report on the health of their businesses. Over time, the money in the bank grew, as did the wealth of the children. The desire that drives many people to leave something behind is to see it become more meaningful than just money. They want to have it impact lives.

Today, if you want to do this properly, you will need a trust. This way you can make sure your wishes and desires are fulfilled with little uncertainty about the actual outcome. Now, if we wanted to make your eyes glaze over and have a blood vessel burst in your head, we would review all the types of trusts you might need. We will save you from that pain. Instead, we will mention two main forms and leave the details to a qualified attorney.

For most situations, you will be fine with a revocable trust. This type of trust allows you to set out want you want to have happen, and it can be changed at any time while you are alive. It becomes set in stone, so to speak, when you pass away. You still own all the assets and can add and remove them if needed. The beauty of a trust is that it avoids probate and cannot be contested like a will.

Also, exactly how and when assets pass is up to you. Assets are a great way to pay for college, weddings, home purchases, and such after you are gone. You can even restrict transfers for bad habits. One of our past clients made the trust require the son to get a drug test every six months before he was given his next six months of income. If he did not pass, he had to wait another six months to pass.

Other times, the circumstances may require you to set up an irrevocable trust. Just as the name indicates, these cannot easily be changed, and more importantly, you lose ownership of any assets transferred into them. When does this type of trust make sense? These come into play primarily when trying to manage estate-tax issues.

If you want to reduce how much of a taxable estate you are leaving, this is a way to do that. A twist on this is the irrevocable life insurance trust, which is like it sounds. You place a life policy inside the trust so that when you die, it does not increase the value of your estate. For many people, this is not currently a problem, but tax laws have been known to change. Take the following example:

- In 1916, the top rate was 10 percent, and the first $50,000 was exempted.
- In 1977, that moved to a top rate of 77 percent and $120,000 exempted.
- In 2010, the estate tax was repealed, only to come back in 2011 with a 35 percent rate and a $5 million exemption.
- In 2017, the tax has a top rate of 40 percent and exempts the first $5,490,000.[1]

The fact of the matter is that what the estate tax will be in the future is unclear. The more the government must pay for, though, the more likely that the estate-tax exemptions will drop as tax rates increase. The best plan is to prepare today as if you will pay a tax. If you have a few large life policies, a successful business, and a house, you might be more exposed than you realize.

Providing continuing oversight is another level of estate planning. We all know someone that is not very good with money, so what happens when he or she inherits a load of cash? New cars, fun parties, new homes, gifts for friends—and the money will evaporate. This is where estate planning can be the most effective. It is possible to control financial matters through a trust to make sure that assets are not squandered and that a beneficiary is taken care of in the best fashion once you are gone.

We provide plenty of ridiculous stories because, when we see them, they are so memorable. However, sometimes the stories involve a very positive purpose, as is the case for families with special-needs children. A special-needs trust allows you peace of mind and the knowledge that your heir will still be provided for after you pass.

Another good reason for using a trust with life insurance is to equalize an estate. The best example is farmers. Imagine a family with four kids. One is still helping work the farm, and the other three are off doing their own things. Dad dies and leaves the farm to all four. For everyone to get what they are due, the farm would have to be sold.

If death occurs in a down year for farmland, everyone gets screwed. If the farmer has bought life insurance, the proceeds can be used to buy out any of the heirs that do not want to farm. That way, the family farm can be maintained, and all the children will be happy. Anyone with a large business or property can benefit from this strategy.

There are other times when a trust makes sense, such as blended families, adoptions, or even secret families. Back in 1997, legendary CBS news reporter Charles Kuralt passed away. At the funeral, his wife learned that Mr. Kuralt had a nearly thirty-year-long relationship with another woman. He had left the mistress property in Montana that she had to go to court to retain.

A trust would have been helpful. OK, so hopefully most of us are not like Chuck here, but it makes the point. If your life has any past issues, bad business deals, or family insanity, you most likely will want a trust.

It is possible to go online and complete a trust. It might be tempting to save some money this way, but don't do it. An online will might be fine, but not a trust. We would stress to you that this is one of those areas where you don't know what you don't know. If you miss significant aspects that need to be in the trust, you can leave your family in even worse shape than if you would have had no trust at all. Getting expert help here can make all the difference in the world.

Once you have completed your planning, you are finished. Well, not exactly. Remember how, at the start of this conversation, we discussed how life rarely works out just like you think it will? A great plan will contain one more piece, regular monitoring.

You will need to revisit your plan and tweak it at least one more time. Anytime there is a death, divorce, marriage, new baby, tax-law change, or other major life event, you will want to go through your plan to see if any changes need to be made. This way, you make sure your legacy is as close to your vision as possible. At times, it is difficult to know the exact right course of action to take. Other times, it is obvious what should be done.

Summary

When it comes to legacy planning, you might need to ask yourself this question: "If I died yesterday, would everything have gone to my heirs the way I wanted it to?" If your answer is not a resounding yes, then you need to put more planning in place.

You can put your estate planning to bed, for now. We opened this chapter by clarifying that every dollar you retire with will either be "Take It" or "Leave It." Keep in mind that if you don't "Leave It" correctly, then your estate could end up looking remarkably similar to a *Game of Thrones* episode. You better swipe left on that one. However, if you want to "Leave It" in a way that preserves your life's work and your family's relationships, then swipe right on leaving a legacy with a great estate plan.

CHAPTER 6

Prepare It

Unfortunately, there seems to be far more opportunity out there than ability...We should remember that good fortune often happens when opportunity meets with preparation.
—Thomas A. Edison, American Inventor

We don't want to take much time here, but knowing how to be ready to meet with a financial coach needs to be discussed, if ever so briefly. You may know the old saying "Garbage in, garbage out." The same can be said when it comes to working with a financial coach. If you do not come prepared with the right items or questions, you will end up getting less money than your financial coach would desire. Unfortunately, no matter how great the coach, he or she can only work with the information that you provide. With that in mind, let's cover how to maximize your meeting time together.

Meeting Preparation and What You'll Need

The meeting process has a few phases, and your financial coach is going to need a certain amount of information to properly assist you with your financial goals. Initially, you need to spend some time thinking about what those specific goals really might be. This preparation is probably one of those times when you should put pen to paper and write your thoughts down.

Have you ever had a conversation where, after you left you, you wished you'd said this or that? Well, a meeting with your financial coach to plan your financial future for the entire rest of your life is not a good time for that to happen. You don't want to leave second-guessing that you omitted an important retirement goal or pertinent piece of information. So thoroughly collect your thoughts, and write them down prior to the meeting.

Be thinking about when you want to retire and how much monthly income you want in retirement. Will you work part time during retirement? Do you have kids or grandkids and want to help with their education expenses? Do you have a big expense coming up, like the purchase of a new home, car, or boat? What does your debt situation look like? Do you have student loans, a mortgage, or big credit-card balances? How much disposable income do you have? How much cash is in your emergency fund?

It is all right if you don't have all the answers or even all the questions. The goal is to try and get an idea of what you think is right, so you and your planner can conduct a meaningful discussion. Also, this is a great time to talk these issues through with your significant other to see where you agree and disagree.

Once you've considered your financial goals, you're probably ready for the next phase of preparation. This is when you will want to prepare for some questions your financial coach is likely to ask you. Remember how your parents taught you that it is rude to ask people their age, how much they weigh, and how much money they have? Well, get ready, because your financial coach is going to ask you all those questions and more to figure out your needs, wants, and circumstances.

Since your financial coach must start somewhere, expect him or her to be curious about your current financial situation. You will be asked about your investment time horizon and risk tolerance. It will be very important for your financial coach to ascertain this information so that appropriately suitable investments can be recommended. As we said before, it is OK if you don't know some of these answers. Your financial coach, whom you need, will help you.

Use the next few charts as a checklist for your meeting preparation.

Checklist: Retirement Goals

❑Basic Living Expenses
❑New Vehicles
❑Health Care
❑Providing Care for Aging Family Members
❑New Home
❑Home Renovations

❑Leave Money to Church, University, Charity, Children, or Family
❑Travel & Vacations
❑Education Expenses for Adult Children or Grandchildren
❑Technology Purchases

Checklist: Assets

❑Employer-Sponsored Plans (SEP, 403(b), 401(k), SIMPLE)
❑Traditional & Roth IRA's
❑Taxable Assets (Stocks, Bonds, Savings, CD's)
❑Tax-Deferred Accounts
❑Tax-Free Accounts

❑529 College Savings
❑Business
❑Home
❑Collectibles & Artwork
❑Personal Property
❑Real Estate
❑Inheritance & Gifts
❑Cash Value Life Insurance

Checklist: Debt and Liabilities

❏Mortgages   ❏Credit Cards
❏Equity Lines of Credit   ❏Personal Lines of Credit
❏Vehicle Loans   ❏Education Expenses
❏Business Loans   ❏Student Loans
❏Medical Loans   ❏Payday Loans

Checklist: Retirement Income Sources

❏Social Security Benefits   ❏Required Minimum
❏Pension Income   Distributions (RMD's)
❏Annuity Income   ❏Cash-Value Life
❏Disability Income   Insurance
❏Alimony   ❏Rental Properties
❏Part-Time Job   ❏Reverse Mortgage
❏Inheritance   ❏Other

Be cognizant of various life events that can impact your financial plan. Changes in status regarding a birth, employment, marriage, and health are notable. Additionally, if you have existing investments, this is a convenient opportunity to review all your beneficiary designations to make sure your money would go where you want it to go if something were to happen to you.

One of the objectives of this second phase is to generally determine if you are on pace to reach your financial goals. You may have to work a little longer than you originally planned or perhaps save a higher percentage of your income each year. By working with your financial coach, you are optimizing your chances to get where you want to go.

Phase three of the meeting process will be designed to move away from an abstract discussion of your financial goals, aspirations, and fears. Now your financial coach is going to get specific and detailed. You are going to need to produce pertinent financial statements, so he or she can get a comprehensive picture of your actual financial situation on which to base portfolio and plan recommendations.

At the end of the process, you should be presented a holistic financial plan encapsulating your needs, wants, and wishes, along with the right path to achieve it all.

If you would like a free financial plan created for you, then visit www.oneretirement.com/2-minute-retirement-checkup and get started by taking the "2 minute" retirement checkup by answering five quick questions. You will be provided with a holistic plan designed to give you the guidance necessary to succeed financially.

Now, just in case you fell asleep or weren't taking good notes, we want to make sure you have a few thoughts to arm yourself with when you go to meet a financial professional to decide if he or she is a swipe left or swipe right.

Use the upcoming Discussion Points checklist for reminders on what to discuss during your interviews with financial professionals.

Current Scenario, Recommended Scenario

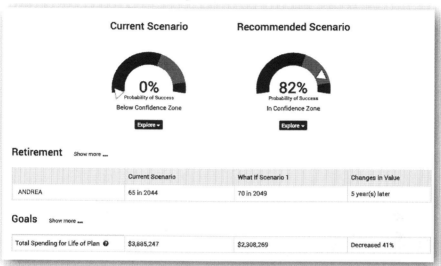

Current Scenario

0%
Probability of Success
Below Confidence Zone

Explore ▾

Recommended Scenario

82%
Probability of Success
In Confidence Zone

Explore ▾

Retirement Show more ...

	Current Scenario	What If Scenario 1	Changes in Value
ANDREA	65 in 2044	70 in 2049	5 year(s) later

Goals Show more ...

Total Spending for Life of Plan ❓	$3,885,247	$2,308,269	Decreased 41%

Discussion Points

❑Tell me about your experiences as a financial advisor.

❑What credentials do you have?

❑What services you do you provide?

❑Tell me about your team.

❑How often can I expect to hear from you?

❑Will you provide me client references?

❑How are you compensated?

❑What are my expenses?

❑Do you have certain company products you are required or encouraged to sell?

❑Tell me about your professional network for legal, tax, and specialty areas.

❑Will you be following the fiduciary standard while advising me?

Also, before you meet with a potential financial coach, you can pull up his or her information on www.FINRA.org, the state insurance website, or at www.sec.gov to make sure he or she has a clean history.

If you are trying to find someone in your area, you can also utilize www.fpanet.org to find a certified financial planner®, the National Association of Personal Financial Advisors (NAPFA) at www.apfa.org, or the Society of Financial Services Professionals at www.financialpro. org.

The goal here is not to run an intense, rapid-fire interrogation. Rather it is to make sure your planner is aligned with all you have learned, as well as to make sure you feel at ease with the person that you will be entrusting your financial stability to moving forward.

Writing a Monthly Spending Plan

You need to brace yourself for the very real possibility that your financial coach is going to give you advice that might be a little uncomfortable. In other words, maybe because of insurability issues, your insurance is going to be more expensive than you'd hoped. Because of lofty retirement goals or a recent bad stock market, your financial plan could dictate that you need to be saving more money (maybe a lot more money) each month than your current savings rate.

There is always the possibility that you may need to tighten your belt temporarily to truly live the lifestyle you desire in retirement. Extra money is not going to magically appear each month for new insurance or retirement-savings needs. Therefore, you would be very wise to put together a written spending plan. That is the best way for you to know you are getting all your bills paid while simultaneously saving enough for retirement.

You can't wing it when it comes to your budget if you genuinely want to build and sustain wealth for the rest of your life. We are not saying you must account for every single penny, which would be tedious for anyone that is not a CPA or engineer. What we are saying is that any successful enterprise has a handle on inflows (your paycheck) and outflows (your expenses).

Some financial coaches will be willing to help you with a written spending plan if you don't already have one. If you want to do one on your own, then there are plenty of useful resources on the Internet that will help you allocate what you earn to make sure those dollars have a purpose, such as www.mint.com.

Don't I Have Another Account with Some Money Over at That One Place?

The title of this section is a very good question. It is a question that you should never want to find yourself asking. As you make good financial decisions, you are going to create wealth. This new wealth is going to increase your net worth. However, it also may make your personal finances more complicated. More accounts with more money in them require you to be more diligent in keeping track of your assets. Think of it like a business needing to keep current tabs on the growing inventory sitting on its shelves.

Once you have a financial plan and a spending plan, you need to write down all your accounts and keep them in a safe place. Our first choice would be to keep a copy in a safety deposit box at your local bank. If you don't want to get a safety deposit box, then at least keep the information in a fireproof safe in your house and make sure the safe is heavy enough that it can't be easily stolen in the event of a home burglary. Another great option is to have your attorney keep the information on file. If you feel safe about keeping information on your computer, then a scanned copy saved on your computer or in the cloud works as well.

The point is that you should have all your financial records in an easily accessible yet extremely safe place. These records should be exhaustive. Don't forget motor-vehicle loans, personal loans, credit cards, insurance policies, homeowner's policies, home-equity loans and mortgages, tangible property, and your other financial accounts.

Use this checklist so you know which information to organize and keep in your safety deposit box:

Checklist: Safety Deposit Box Organization

❑Name of Financial Institution and Phone Number

❑Account Owner(s)

❑Account Number(s)

❑Copy of Will, Trust, & Estate Plan Documents

❑Website Addresses with User Names & Passwords

❑Attorney's Contact Information

❑Accountant's Contact Information

❑Financial Coach's Contact Information

This list will greatly aid your beneficiaries or estate in the event something untimely happens to you. It will also keep you from ever asking, "Don't I have another account with some money over at that one place?" That's because you'll know right where your money is. You'll already have most of your homework completed when you get ready to do your next annual review. That's it. Now you are ready. Go take advantage of the opportunities that lie ahead, and "Prepare It!"

CHAPTER 7
CHOOSE IT

There's always one more thing you can do to influence any
situation in your favor—and after that one more thing, and
after that...The more you do the more opportunities arise.
—HAROLD G. (HAL) MOORE, LIEUTENANT GENERAL,
US ARMY, DISTINGUISHED SERVICE CROSS RECIPIENT, AND
AUTHOR OF *WE WERE SOLDIERS ONCE...AND YOUNG*

Now it is time to choose your financial-coaching match. Several years ago, Morningstar Inc. did a research study on investors and determined that working with a financial coach generated 31 percent more retirement income. Morningstar says, "The true risk for a retirement portfolio is not the standard deviation of the asset portfolio. Rather, it is the risk that you won't be able to meet your spending goals."[1]

Meeting these spending goals is more likely if a financial coach helps you achieve total wealth-asset allocation, a dynamic withdrawal strategy, proper annuity allocation, tax efficiency through asset allocation and withdrawal sequencing, liability-relative optimization, and Social Security maximization.

Take note that none of those value-adds involve market timing or a pure return model. A talented financial coach doesn't provide his or her value that way. It comes through meaningful behavioral coaching. This guidance makes all the difference.

Vanguard, the gargantuan no-load mutual fund and ETF manager, went even further than Morningstar by releasing an exhaustive report discussing the myriad of reasons a financial coach is necessary to an investor's success. Vanguard estimates that a skillful financial coach's impact from good advice generates a net additional investor gain of 3 percent.

Vanguard comes to that number by showing that the financial coach generates 4 percent additional growth, minus a 1 percent fee for that guidance. The report describes that the excess performance comes from an experienced financial coach building a customized investment plan. The well-constructed plan is aimed at achieving goals and meeting constraints for risk tolerance and risk capacity, minimizing risks and tax impacts, and providing coaching on behavioral issues.[2]

Justin Wagner from Vanguard offers the following example: "Suppose the overall market return is 8 percent. Without good financial decision-making, the combined impact of fees, taxes, and poor investment decisions is around 4 percent. This leaves a net return of 4 percent for the investor. But someone working with a capable coach eliminates poor investment decisions, minimizes taxes, and only pays the 1 percent fee, leaving a net return of 7 percent. That is the Coach Alpha."[3]

Providing an additional 3 percent compounded each year for the rest of your life could make a seven-figure difference in your future net worth. But where did that number come from? Investors might understand it in the abstract, but what about specifics? Check out this chart for the breakdown in Vanguard's study.

Vanguard Advisor Value

Alpha Strategy Modules	Value-Add Relative to "Avg." Client Experience
Asset Allocation using Broadly Diversified Funds/ETFS	> 0 bps
Cost-Effective Implementation (Expense Ratios)	45 bps
Rebalancing	35 bps
Behavioral Coaching	150 bps
Asset Allocation	75 bps
Spending Strategy (Withdrawal Order)	70 bps
Total Return vs. Income Investing	> 0 bps
Potential Value Added:	About 4%

Source: Vanguard

The study shows the value-add compared to the average client experience. Understanding this chart requires you to know that one hundred basis points (bps) equals 1 percent. So, twenty-five bps then equals 0.25 percent or one-quarter of 1 percent.

Choosing suitable asset allocation using the right broadly diversified mutual funds or ETFs matters. It represents something above zero bps, but it is too hard to quantify on an individual investor basis. Being smart about expenses is worth about forty-five bps annually. Rebalancing effectively is worth thirty-five bps, and behavioral coaching is a notable 150 bps.

As we discussed in "Grow It," asset allocation matters and is valued at about seventy-five bps. Knowing the right way to withdraw your money as income in retirement is worth up to seventy bps. Collectively, this represents close to 4 percent in return before advisory fees are assessed.

Under the heading "What have you done for me lately?" we would add that even further compelling research has been completed since the Vanguard study. Goldman Sachs looked at portfolios that included emerging market equities, emerging market debt, and international small-cap equities.[4]

After researching the findings, ONE Retirement's Ron Sanders wrote, "Portfolios with all three diversifying asset classes experienced higher annualized returns (6.8 percent compared to 6.1 percent) for virtually the same level of risk—10.8 percent annualized volatility for portfolios with all three asset classes, compared to 10.7 percent for those which excluded all three."[5]

Moreover, New York City–based Betterment LLC researched the effects of a properly dedicated tax-coordinated portfolio. Betterment's conclusion was that a portfolio correctly allocated across taxable, tax-deferred, and tax-exempt accounts can increase performance by forty-eight bps annually.[6] That additional tax savings could add 15 percent to a client's portfolio over a thirty-year period.[7]

What is the takeaway? It is that an experienced financial coach can design a portfolio for you that may increase your net returns beyond the 3 percent or 4 percent that even Vanguard established several years back.

The numbers are downright predictable if you really think about it. Haven't we been talking about behavior this entire book? The numbers make perfect sense. Two factors that significantly impact being a successful lifetime investor are keeping a laser-like focus on the things you can control while at the same time keeping a proper perspective on the things you cannot control. A good financial coach will assist you in maximizing good decisions while helping you navigate your emotions to minimize bad decisions.

Let's start with what you can't control. Neither you nor your financial coach has any control over the stock market's performance, the sequence or order of that performance, whether interest rates go up or down (or when), the unemployment rate, whether the economy expands or contracts, or even what future tax laws will be. You can see that making bold predictions on the future can be precarious.

The good news is that the things you and your financial coach can control are what make nearly all the difference. Do you need long-term care insurance, and if so, what type? Which retirement accounts will provide you the most bang for your buck? What is the proper legacy plan so that your kids and church get your money instead of the government? How effectively are you leveraged for a worst-case scenario?

The list keeps going. Are you planning for tax efficiency not just today but also when you are in retirement? Which income-distribution model will provide you the highest level of emotional and financial security? Are you taking advantage of the most effective ways to save for a college education? Do you have a Social Security strategy that ensures you can potentially receive 132 percent of your benefit instead of merely 70 percent?

Some of these examples are broad and intangible, while others are very narrow, specific, and measurable. But they all go to the point of how much more wealth you will create and preserve by collaborating with a financial coach. Your financial professional will help you build a well-thought-out plan that accomplishes all your goals.

In the meantime, you will have peace of mind in knowing that you seized the initiative on all the things you can control. Taking control of your financial future, with the help of your financial coach, will quite possibly change your family's financial situation for a generation or more. We know that value far exceeds the amount you'll be paying in fees. In fact, that fee might just be the bargain of a lifetime.

Discerning between a Financial Coach and a Mere Product Salesman

The challenge ahead of you is to continuously make sound financial decisions. That's a big task. You are going to need a strong financial coach to guide you along the way. Spend some time thinking about the characteristics you might want in a financial professional. Remember, you are the client; it is your financial life being planned. We have accumulated numerous stories and anecdotes over the years. We will share some of them with you, so you can discern whether the person you are interviewing is a comprehensive financial coach or merely a product salesman.

It is usually easy for a financial professional to see when something is right or wrong. In fact, oftentimes advisors can readily spot shortcomings in other advisors or insurance agents. However, it isn't always so easy for financial professionals to recognize those same flaws in themselves. Sometimes in our consulting, we come across insurance agents and advisors who are product salesmen because they just don't understand the value of proper planning.

Let's get started with a few stories, keeping in mind that the names and places have been changed to protect both the innocent and the not so innocent. This first one would be funny if it weren't true. It happened when we were asked to help an insurance agent set up a retirement plan for a small business.

The agent's insurance company had announced internally that it was exiting the retirement-plan business and that all existing clients would keep their plans, but only on a self-directed basis—meaning they wouldn't be receiving any further investment help. However, the investing public did not yet widely know this change. Since the company had not officially shut down retirement planning, the agent wanted to move forward with plan implementation.

In 2016 the US Department of Labor prepared for the implementation of a new Fiduciary Rule, which was set to go into effect in 2017. The rule will place a significantly higher level of accountability for financial professionals when it comes to providing advice and services for any kind of retirement accounts, such as IRAs. In response to the new rule, the insurance agent said, "I don't know what the big deal is; if agents would just do the right thing, then it seems like it would be easy to follow the new Fiduciary Rule." We agreed! That made sense. So far so good.

Now here's where it got ridiculous. In prepping for the client's arrival, we asked the agent how he wanted to handle the discussion about the insurance company leaving the mutual-fund business. The agent paused and then nonchalantly said, "I guess in all my years of selling, I've learned that sometimes you can just say too much, and then that just sort of muddies the waters, you know?"

We thought that was a stunning insight into the mind of a salesman. The truth is that a good financial coach isn't worried about muddying the waters. Rather, he or she is worried that you have all the information you need to make the right decision. We were thinking that this agent's mentality was quite literally the reason the Department of Labor wrote the new rule. However, the agent had no idea that he was part of the problem.

Put yourself in this situation. If you were talking to someone who was promising you a service, you would assume he or she would be around long enough to provide the service all the way through to completion. If the agent knew beforehand that he or she wouldn't be able to properly fulfill the service, you would expect that information to be disclosed. You would then be able to decide if this was such a good deal that you still wanted to move forward or if you wanted go in a different direction.

Financial-services professionals are required to regularly take ethics courses to keep up to date with securities and insurance requirements. Somewhere in those courses, the subject matter will address the concept of moral perception. If your financial professional possesses moral perception, then he or she will be aware of morally relevant facts.

The study of applied ethics is basically learning how to apply your morals and values to a situation. The salesman above clearly didn't apply this concept. That fear of losing the sale kept him from behaving at the highest ethical level.

Have you ever been in a situation in your career or personal life where you were surrounded by "crazy," but then after you had been there so long, it became the new normal? Eventually, you just got sucked in and were desensitized to the outrageous carnival encircling you, so you forgot how to be normal. That phenomenon can happen to insurance agents and advisors if they get caught up in behaviors and attitudes that don't remain solely focused on successful client outcomes.

The next client, Susie, had a modest 401(k) account but wasn't contributing up to her company's match. She came in with financial-planning needs, including life insurance and investment planning. Susie's budget should have been a factor in knowing which goals to prioritize. The salesman's solution was to use a permanent cash-value life-insurance policy to meet all three needs simultaneously.

A good financial coach, though, would help Susie prioritize her goals to fit within her available budget for insurance and investments. As an example, a term-insurance policy would be a less expensive solution while also allowing for the creation of an emergency fund. Knowing that Susie is giving up free money in her 401(k), she should have been advised to contribute up to the full company match.

Remember our story about the Ginsu knives? The moral of that story is that salespeople become indoctrinated to believe a particular product is always the best. Usually the indoctrination comes from the company that hires the salesperson into the industry. He or she is trained on what product the company is especially wanting sold, not necessarily what was the best for the client. The biases a salesperson learns first make it difficult to break free from a product-oriented mind-set later in his or her career.

A good financial coach will have addressed this issue through an independent business model, meaningful education, and professional growth. You need to seek out a financial coach with a thorough education background. You need the confidence that your coach will know what to do once he or she has learned about your financial situation, your goals, and your fears.

Having trust about your financial coach's competence is critical. A successful coach today should know how all the various aspects of your financial needs should be balanced with one another as well as understanding the tax ramifications today and in the future of the different tools that will be implemented.

In many careers, including financial services, there are opportunities for growing your knowledge base. During a coach's professional career, there are many opportunities to continuously learn and adapt. You wouldn't want your next surgical procedure to be done by a doctor who is still using 1990s ideas and technology, would you? We didn't think so. Likewise, you should insist on finding a financial coach who has demonstrated an eagerness to improve.

Three great examples for professional development are CFP®, RICP®, and AIF® designations. The CFP® is earned from the CFP® Board of Standards Inc. The American College standardizes the RICP®, while Fi360 oversees the AIF® program.

CFP® stands for certified financial planner and is recognized as a "standard of excellence for competent and ethical financial planning."[8] The RICP® stands for retirement income certified professional and intensely "focuses on transitioning from asset accumulation to creating a sustainable livelihood for clients in retirement."[9] Fi360's mission is to ensure the use of "prudent fiduciary practices to profitably gather, grow, and protect investors' assets."[10]

There is certainly no mandatory requirement for a coach to have a financial designation. These designations are very difficult and time-consuming to attain, to say the least. However, it does offer evidence that your coach takes his or her career very seriously if he or she has done something significant to further his or her education. You can use that evidence to decipher whether your financial professional has done enough to separate him- or herself from a product-centered mentality. Go ahead and swipe right on a well-educated financial coach.

Education is not the only aspect you need to consider when trying to find the right person. The next thing you should look for is whether your financial coach is approachable. Why do clients sometimes withhold financial information or not give their advisors a full picture of their situations? There are several reasons, usually including that the necessary trust hasn't been established.

A red flag that you might be in a salesperson situation is if you're being asked to complete application paperwork on your first or second meeting. On the other hand, a solid financial coach will be amicable, make you feel at ease, and invest the necessary time to build two-way trust. If these criteria are met, then you'll give him or her the necessary information to build the correct financial plan. And keep in mind that a financial coach can only help you based upon the information you provide.

Meetings with your financial coach are not a time to be bashful. You can swipe right if you find an approachable financial coach who cares about your situation and whom you feel comfortable talking to about delicate matters.

In recent years, the various ways financial professionals are compensated has come under increased scrutiny. If your financial coach efficiently solves your problems or designs a great financial plan for you, then you probably don't care much how he or she gets paid. The only time it becomes an issue is when there is no apparent value. But it is good to understand how people get paid nevertheless.

A very common form of revenue for a financial professional is to be paid commissions by an insurance or investment company based upon the products you, the client, purchase. Another possibility is to be paid fees for giving advice, managing money, or designing financial plans. Typically, the commissions are based upon the premiums paid or amount invested, whereas fees are based upon the ongoing assets under management (AUM). Less frequently, fees are assessed on an hourly or flat rate.

Be aware that this is an area where marketing comes into play. Financial advisors who are fee only like to talk about how charging fees is the better model for the client, while financial professionals who are structured around commission sales will suggest that their approach is better. Due to how different financial products work, the truth is somewhere in the middle.

As a consumer, you should be aware that there is a significant trend in the industry toward fee-only planning, especially inside IRAs and 401(k)s. The Department of Labor Fiduciary Rule has aggressively accelerated this trend. It is plausible that in the relatively near future, there will no longer be any commission-type business being handled inside retirement accounts. Instead, the products offered will be fee based.

Our preference is for financial professionals to be fee based when it comes to investable assets. It is much easier to understand what you are being charged when it is a straight fee or a fee calculated as a percentage of your assets. We believe the full transparency offered by such an approach is an essential client benefit.

However, we are not always opposed to commissionable products, and in certain scenarios there may be no other option. An example would be for the person that needs the investing parachutes. If the proper choice is to use a variable annuity, the financial coach may have no option but to use a commission-based product.

The same can be said for an income-annuity or life-insurance product. Our hope is that with recent industry changes, the big insurance companies realize the value of designing products that are low cost and fit well into a fee-based model. Increased transparency in costs for insurance products would be a win for everyone involved.

How a financial planner is compensated regarding fees versus commissions isn't the real issue. *The core issue is whether they owe you a fiduciary duty or not.* We'll discuss this concept deeper in a little bit and make it clear why you should care about it. For now, it is important to remember that some financial products only offer the financial coach fee-based compensation, while other financial products only offer commission compensation.

A secondary issue is how the financial coach, in terms of method, gets paid. However, it is very pertinent to know what you are actually paying, in terms of total price. Be on the lookout for what your overall costs end up being. You need to do your due diligence to ensure you aren't paying for unnecessary things.

The fee-and-compensation conversation is a discussion where a salesperson will try to skim the surface. A financial coach, in sharp contrast, will voluntarily disclose everything you need to know. Then he or she will go the extra mile to ensure you know what you are paying and why.

It should be a major red flag if your advisor seems unwilling or unable to succinctly answer any and every question about your fees or his or her compensation. You will want to swipe right if you meet a financial coach who thoroughly educates you on all your expenses.

Impact of Fees over Thirty Years

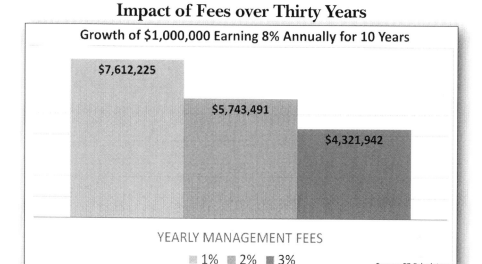

Growth of $1,000,000 Earning 8% Annually for 10 Years

$7,612,225

$5,743,491

$4,321,942

YEARLY MANAGEMENT FEES

1% 2% 3%

Source: EZ Calculators

Let's tie the fiduciary-and-compensation conversation together now with a specific instance. Sometimes insurance companies and broker dealers set up sales contests and incentive plans that increase sales but decrease focus on client outcomes. When this conflict of interest occurs, the company places tremendous pressure on the salesperson to make transactional sales.

Some insurance companies place high numbers of life-insurance applications as a requirement for bonuses and travel awards. If the salesperson doesn't sell something like sixty or seventy new life cases annually, then he or she won't qualify for the company award trip.

When the salesperson is pressured to focus on transactions, the result is more transaction-based business and less client-outcome-focused business. When we see $25,000 permanent-life policies and $100,000 term-life policies across the board, then we know with certainty that this is a transaction-focused business. In what world does every client need the same insurance coverage? The answer is a world where insurance-coverage priorities aren't reconciled with client needs.

Here is a quick example of this transaction-based sales model. Sometimes salespeople excessively submit multiple life-insurance applications on the same client even though it would be more efficient to just write one. One proposed contract might be a $125,000 term-life policy for $27 a month. The second suggested contract is a $10,000 permanent-life policy for $73 monthly. The total coverage is $135,000.

Is that a good deal? Well, compared to what? The client could buy over $300,000 in death benefits if the salesperson instead writes one term policy with the same premium instead of this expensive combination.

Hold on—here's the punch line: The salesperson submits the applications sixty-one days apart because the insurance company had a rule where life applications taken at the same time, but submitted over sixty days apart, count for two life applications instead of just one. We hope you are thinking, "Swipe left!" right now.

Don't be afraid to ask your insurance professional if your insurance policy is being counted toward a travel conference or awards trip. If a salesperson selling you an insurance policy will earn an extra bonus at the end of the year, then you have a right to know about that potential conflict of interest. A salesperson getting credit for more life applications makes you a statistic and not a client. Feel free to swipe left and instead seek out a good financial coach elsewhere.

In this same vein, be wary of an advisor showing you products only from the company for whom he or she works. Insurance companies and broker dealers may offer proprietary products that they would prefer you purchase. If that is all that is being shown to you, then excuse yourself for a second opinion elsewhere before making a final purchasing decision.

Nearly all great financial coaches offer a wide range of investments from many companies. They can get you a first, second, and third opinion with their collaborative efforts. But be prepared to swipe left if you only see proprietary product proposals.

A trend in the financial-services industry is that some professionals are beginning to give up their securities licenses and only keep their state insurance licenses. The motivation behind this shift is decreased regulatory costs and oversight. This issue is going to continue to grow in the years to come, so you really need to understand this point.

To be clear, selling fixed annuities, index annuities, or nonvariable life insurance only requires a state insurance license. Selling these products does not legally require a securities license. But practically speaking, as a consumer of financial products and financial-planning services, you must be careful about working with non-securities-licensed professionals.

Why is this point so important? The answer is because when you roll your 401(k) mutual funds into an IRA, your insurance agent might recommend purchasing a fixed or index annuity since that may be all he or she can sell. He or she might also recommend that you sell equities and use the proceeds to purchase life insurance. It is hard to believe that someone that can provide only a portion of the options available can always be putting your best interests first.

The crux of the issue is that if the insurance professional is not licensed to sell a mutual fund to you, then he or she may not be qualified to advise you to redeem that mutual fund to buy an annuity or life insurance. He or she may be an expert in the annuity details, but if he or she is not licensed to offer the 401(k) or IRA account holdings you are liquidating, then it will be an uphill climb to know the pros and cons.

The truth is that we could probably fill an entire book on all the ways we have seen it done wrong by salespeople. Our point is to help you see the difference between the better way and the wrong way. The thing to always keep in your mind is that if the person sitting across from you displays the proper behaviors (yes, advisors have emotional issues too), that will help you identify a coach versus a salesperson. From here on, we will focus on what a true financial coach will look like.

Think of great coaches or mentors you have had the privilege of knowing at some point in your life. The qualities they possess, such as knowing who you really are, what motivates you, and what worries you, and even telling you what you don't want to hear—these are the same traits to look for in a financial coach.

When people get stressed, they get irrational, and there will be times in the years ahead where the planning process stresses you out. A financial coach will possess the skills to lead you through those challenging times, which will make a huge difference.

When significant family events occur and troubling financial events transpire, you will want someone in whom you can trust as well as confide. If you are hesitant to be open with a financial coach, just understand that it can make his or her job harder. A great coach will want what is best for you, but he or she must know what your situation truly is.

Another way to identify a financial coach is to see if he or she is surrounded by a great team. Financial coaches who work alone tend to miss things. That doesn't mean there aren't great financial coaches who can work alone. But it is usually desirable to be surrounded by people whom you can bounce ideas off and brainstorm with on complicated financial-planning issues. It is basically impossible for one person to be an expert on all areas of your financial life. A team approach fixes that issue.

Another advantage for you with the team approach is there should be a continuation plan in place for when the advisor retires, dies, or becomes disabled. All the time we hear clients say, "My guy retired, and now there's a new guy that I got a letter about who is taking care of my accounts." That's terrible, folks.

Here are the behind-the-scenes politics of how that works. An agent or advisor gets fired or retires, and the insurance-company office manager or broker-dealer principal now must assign all those accounts to a different representative. They will likely do one of two things.

First, they may assign your account to the least-experienced advisors, who need the most help staying in the business. That's not an optimal way for an investor to end up with a financial planner who is responsible for coaching a client toward a lifetime of good financial decisions.

Second, in every office, there are manager favorites and not-so-favorites. There's a high probability that your new "guy" is part of the good-ole-boy-or-girl network. The truth is that you must make sure you are working with an advisor based solely upon his or her skill and ability to help you reach your financial goals. Make sure you ask your financial coach if he or she has a client-continuation plan, and then meet the people involved.

Along those same lines, a financial coach will also use a collaborative approach. We know this approach is a positive trend for investors. More perspectives create environments where the best ideas come to the top, along with accountability to peers. Legal, tax, portfolio design, and product knowledge are just a few of the ways a financial coach can work collaboratively with other professionals.

A few things to look for would be whether coaches use insurance or investment-company wholesalers to help teach them different products, whether they have financial-coach partners, or whether they have access to excellent training and support staff. Are they part of a professional organization, and what are the values of that group? Are they aligned with an attorney, mortgage consultant, and CPA who can be leaned on for quick tax, mortgage, and legal updates? These are questions you should always be asking.

Another thing to consider is the way in which the financial professional is licensed and registered. That's remarkably understating it. We especially want to emphasize this point. You must choose a financial coach who owes you, the client, a fiduciary duty.

That's legal jargon for stating that the financial coach is legally and ethically obligated to *always* put the client's interests above his or her own, regardless of what type of work he or she is doing for you. The true test is if the coach goes beyond the baseline by ensuring your solutions not only include all of your numbers, but have considered your values, beliefs, and behaviors. Keep reading, and we'll expound on the reasons.

This fiduciary standard, like fancy $1,100 Bose headphones, blocks out all the unwanted noise and enhances the sounds you want to hear. Investors have no idea how much of the noise they hear is merely marketing. Do you want mutual funds or variable annuities? What investors don't understand is that this question is just like asking, "Do you want Coke or Pepsi?"

Insurance companies who don't sell mutual funds desperately want you to buy variable annuities. The reason? Because it is what they sell. Mutual-fund companies who don't sell variable annuities keenly want you to buy mutual funds—because it is what they sell.

So be very wary of advisors who make exclusionary claims such as, "I only do life insurance and annuities," or "I only do mutual funds." If an advisor has set his or her financial-planning practice up to favor only a certain product line, then there's going to exist a potential conflict of interest. This moral hazard is what has caused the US Department of Labor to issue new rules that require a fiduciary standard on all 401(k) and IRA advice.

Why You Must Care about the Fiduciary Standard
Only time will tell us the ultimate fate of the Department of Labor's Fiduciary Rule. It could be enforced, strengthened, or weakened.

Additionally, the Securities and Exchange Commission (SEC) may adopt some version of the rule going forward. We have absolute confidence that this genie is out of the bottle. Whether it happens this year or during a future presidential administration, there is going to be increased scrutiny on how financial advisors function.

When you think fiduciary standard, be aware that it requires your advisor act in your best interests. Period. Like an attorney who must always represent his or her client in a manner that is best for the client, an investment-advisor representative (IAR) affiliated with a registered-investment-advisor (RIA) firm and charging a fee must always put his or her client's needs ahead of everything else.

The IAR's highest fiduciary duty is to always put the client first, so don't compromise on this point. The fiduciary standard liberates your advisor. It frees your advisor from worrying about his or her own compensation or what his or her employer prefers.

Imagine a physician without constraints from what health-insurance companies require for reimbursements and coverage. That's a financial coach operating under the fiduciary standard. It's a person who only cares about your portfolio's health and you.

The other legal standard is called the suitability standard. When you think suitability standard, think sales. It is the standard that salespeople follow under compulsion to know the client. The hope is that this standard will prevent an unsuitable investment from being sold.

But mere hope isn't a legal requirement. Like we suggested earlier, you don't need to care if your financial coach is being compensated with commissions rather than fees. You need to care if he or she owes you a fiduciary standard. That is the essential fact you must understand. Feel free to swipe right if your financial coach is required to abide by the fiduciary standard.

Product Complexity

Products and services in the financial world continue to change at a rapid pace. Some of today's most popular product features and management strategies didn't even exist in the late 1990s. Not only are offerings new, but they have also become more complex. It is implausible that investors could do their own full-time jobs and deal with all that life throws at them while still keeping tabs on all the financial products available. It is very difficult to properly assess the risks associated with the financial products available for purchase today. Outsourcing that responsibility to a financial coach is going to stack the deck in your favor.

Somewhere in the complexity discussion is a scenario where an investor has a relative who sells some insurance on the side, an adult son, daughter, or neighbor who will say something like, "I heard the no-load XYZ Mutual Fund is something you should roll your 401(k) into. That and some cheap term insurance is all you need."

In all levels of society, it is admirable to be aware of fees. Remember, though, cost is only an issue in the absence of value. Building a portfolio with the right products, diversification, income options, and asset allocation is complex.

We would wonder whether any of those backseat driver folks giving you advice could tell you what the alpha and the beta are for that recommended fund? Or what the maximum drawdown is? Or how about the Sharpe ratio? Or if adding that new fund changes the standard deviation of your retirement plan? Or how they all correlate to one another? Or why all of that even matters?

Most likely your do-it-yourself neighbors will not have even heard of these terms. All they know is some guy on the radio said you should have no-load investments. Therefore, the cheap no-load XYZ Mutual Fund must be the best. But again, cost is only an issue in the absence of value. And that value is in working with a financial coach.

OK, Fine—I Get It. But Is a Financial Coach Really Worth It?

What was the first main topic we covered? That's right, "Plan it." With a plan, your success increases significantly. When it comes to your money's success, that is even truer. A professional financial plan is imperative to reaching your goals. You must have an ongoing legitimate benchmark and be able to monitor your progress.

When you and your financial coach sit down and figure out how to best reach your retirement goals, only your financial plan will be able to guide you. There is no way to avoid it, and there is no shortcut. Otherwise, in all likelihood, you will start to compare your progress to the current state of the economy, to your neighbor's finances, or to whatever the S&P 500 is doing this year. None of those things matter to you. The only thing that matters is your financial well-being.

You simply must remain disciplined. Disciplined to what? Disciplined to your financial plan. Discipline will keep you doing the things you need to do and prevent you from doing the things you shouldn't. Recall that nearly every financial mistake is made by doing the wrong thing at the wrong moment with the wrong rationale.

Specifically, there are several ways you can invest with good discipline. You are always going to need peace of mind. Neither you nor your financial coach can control the unexpected, but he or she can put together a plan that can weather the storms and get you to your goals. Along with your disciplined investment behavior, you should have greater financial peace of mind than you imagined you would.

Patience is critical to getting it right. You might want to get impatient when you see a particular index, stock, or market sector really begin to outperform everything else. This is a time to sit back and remember that your benchmark is not a particular index, like the S&P 500; or a stock, like Apple (AAPL); or a sector, like pharmaceuticals. Each of the components of your portfolio is there for a reason. Think about those reasons, and whenever necessary, call your financial coach and let him or her remind you of why you chose the course you are on and why the plan is still valid.

There were eight bear markets during the forty-five years from 1970 to 2015. Those forty-five years saw an average of at least one 20 percent drop every 5.6 years. If you or your spouse lives a twenty-five-year retirement (and the odds say you will), then that means if the next twenty-five years are anything like the past forty-five years, you might be looking at another four to five bear markets during your retirement. This fact is not something you should fear. It is something your financial coach can help you prepare for, so when it happens, you don't have to worry.

Remember, in between each of those bear markets were torrid bull markets that have created more wealth than any country has ever seen in the history of the world. The members of the greatest generation lived through the Great Depression. Because they shared their stories, this experienced impacted not only them, but their kids and grandkids as well. All of us have heard stories of what is was like back then.

While most of us can't relate to that time period directly, we all did just live through the Great Recession. Here are some striking numbers that, believe it or not, should give you peace of mind. The Dow Jones Industrial Average (DJIA) and the S&P 500 peaked on October 9, 2007. The Nasdaq peaked the following day.

You remember what happened next; we suffered through a very turbulent and ugly bear market filled with bad news and scary headlines. The next seventeen months saw huge market drops until eventually the DJIA, S&P 500, and the Nasdaq finally bottomed out. The Nasdaq dropped 54.9 percent, the S&P lost 56.6 percent, and the DJIA fell 53.9 percent as of March 9, 2009, from their respective highs seventeen months prior.

Then they began to recover. They didn't just recover—they launched into what became the third longest bull market in US history. The market has reached new all-time highs even after the dot-com bubble, 9/11, and the catastrophic mortgage crisis and housing bubble. The markets giveth, and the markets taketh away. A good plan has that all built into it, knowing that market fluctuation will happen again and again and again. And then probably again after that.

A solid financial coach focused on your financial goals will help you remember that the main idea is not outperforming your neighbor's investments. Rather the main goal is to not run out of money and to give you the best chance possible of living a dignified retirement doing the things you enjoy. If Steve runs out of money in his early eighties but Sally doesn't run out of money until her late eighties, it won't make much difference if they are both ninety and broke.

So where does that leave us? Right back at the beginning. Despite all the facts and examples that we have provided, it still comes back to one essential challenge. We as people tend to let emotions dictate our actions. We're sure that by now you see that the best thing you can do is to figure out how to combat those emotions.

One of our favorite TV shows is the *Biggest Loser*. It is great to see people be given the opportunity to overcome a monumental emotional obstacle. Most people do not become overweight due to a desire to eat excessively. They usually eat to comfort a psychological problem.

However, that is not the main reason we, the authors, like the show. We like how each coach over the years has taken a different approach, yet they are all doing the same thing. They make sure that the contestants stay on the right path. All good coaches know that the path to success is usually pretty simple.

For example, the way to lose weight is to eat right and exercise—simple. The discipline to do those two simple tasks is where it gets hard. A great coach will do whatever it takes to keep you on the right path. That is no less true when it comes to your finances.

Do you want to hedge against being your own worst enemy? You need an excellent financial coach. Hiring a great financial coach will help you swipe left on bad advice and swipe right when it is time to plan and reach your financial dreams.

ABOUT THE AUTHORS

D aniel A. Jack, JD, MBA, RICP®, has worked in both commission and fee-based financial planning fields, including working as a wholesaler for Jackson National Life Distributors and as the west-central zone director for New York Life Insurance.

Jack served a term in the Kansas legislature and as the state securities commissioner. He now represents ONE Retirement, LLC. He has two daughters and volunteers as a children's puppeteer and Sunday School teacher.
www.linkedin.com/in/danielajackjdmba
@DanielAJack87

Derek E. Woods, CFP®, entered the world of financial services in 2000. A certified financial planner, Woods has extensive experience and has conducted educational presentations for clients, Fortune 500 companies, cultural markets, NAIFA, and financial professionals as well.

Woods lives in the great state of Colorado with his amazing wife and his two teenage sons.
www.linkedin.com/in/derek-woods-cfp-%C2%AE-91b1665
@Dewitmoneycoach

REFERENCES

Chapter 1: Plan It

1. "The Future of Retirement: The Power of Planning." HSBC (July 2011): 4. https://www.us.hsbc.com/1/PA_1_083Q9FJ08A002FBP5S00000000/content/usshared/Personal%20Services/Other%20Services/Retirement/Default/FOR_09132011.pdfId.
2. "The Future of Retirement: The Power of Planning." HSBC (July 2011): 35. https://www.expat.hsbc.com/1/PA_ES_Content_Mgmt/content/hsbc_expat/pdf/en/wealth/reports/futureofretirementreport.pdf.
3. Ibid., 40.
4. Tom Hegna. *Don't Worry, Retire Happy! Seven Steps to Retirement Security.* KQED Television (San Francisco, CA: April 2016).
5. "The Future of Retirement: The Power of Planning." HSBC (July 2011): 2. https://www.us.hsbc.com/1/PA_1_083Q9FJ08A002FBP5S00000000/content/usshared/Personal%20Services/Other%20Services/Retirement/Default/FOR_09132011.pdfId.
6. Ibid., 4.
7. Ibid.
8. "The Future of Retirement: The Power of Planning." HSBC (July 2011): 35.

https://www.expat.hsbc.com/1/PA_ES_Content_Mgmt/content/hsbc_expat/pdf/en/wealth/reports/futureofretirementreport.pdf.
9. Ibid.
10. Ibid.
11. Ibid.
12. Ibid.
13. Ibid., 4.
14. Ibid.
15. Ibid.
16. Ibid.
17. Stephanie R. Summers. "Financial Planning Basics." (December 2011). http://www.thecmlink.com/wordpress/wp-content/uploads/allfiles/wealthmanagement/personalfinance/recentarticles/2011%20-%20December%20-%20Financial%20Planning%20Basics%20-%20Kramer%20Financial.pdf.
18. "The Future of Retirement: The Power of Planning." HSBC (July 2011): 38. https://www.expat.hsbc.com/1/PA_ES_Content_Mgmt/content/hsbc_expat/pdf/en/wealth/reports/futureofretirementreport.pdf.
19. Ibid.
20. Ibid.
21. Ibid., 49.
22. Derek Johnson. "Ninety Percent of Text Messages Are Read Within Three Minutes." (April 2012). http://www.tatango.com/blog/90-of-text-messages-are-read-within-3-minutes/.

Chapter 2: Grow It

1. Brad Barber and Terrance Odean, "Trading Is Hazardous to Your Wealth," *Journal of Finance* LV, no. 2 (April 2000): 773. http://faculty.haas.berkeley.edu/odean/papers/returns/Individual_Investor_Performance_Final.pdf.
2. Charles D. Ellis, *Winning the Loser's Game: Timeless Strategies for Successful Investing* (McGraw Hill Education NY, NY, 2013).

3. Brad Barber and Terrance Odean, "Trading Is Hazardous to Your Wealth," *Journal of Finance* LV, no. 2 (April 2000): 773. http://faculty.haas.berkeley.edu/odean/papers/returns/Individual_Investor_Performance_Final.pdf.

4. Shlomo Benartzi, "Behavioral Finance in Action: Psychological Challenges in the Financial Advisor/Client Relationship, and Strategies to Solve Them." (May 2012). http://befi.allianzgi.com/en/Publications/Documents/Part%202-%20Investor%20Paralysis.pdf.

5. Dan Ariely, *Predictably Irrational: The Hidden Forces That Shape Our Decisions*, Revised and Expanded Edition (New York: Harper Perennial, 2010).

6. D. Kahneman and A. Tversky, "Prospect Theory: An Analysis of Decision under Risk," *Econometrica* 47 (1979): 263–291.

7. Charles P. Kindleberger, *Manias, Panics and Crashes: A History of Financial Crises* (Hoboken, New Jersey: Wiley, 2000).

8. "Spatial Disorientation: Visual Illusions." Federal Aviation Administration (January 2000). http://www.faa.gov/pilots/safety/pilotsafetybrochures/media/SpatialD_Seeing.pdf.

9. "NTSB Releases Final Report on Investigation of Crash of Aircraft Piloted by John F. Kennedy Jr." National Transportation Safety Board Office of Public Affairs (July 2000). http://www.ntsb.gov/news/press-releases/Pages/NTSB_NTSB_releases_final_report_on_investigation_of_crash_of_aircraft_piloted_by_John_F._Kennedy_Jr.aspx.

10. Joe Tomlinson, "The Best Solution for Protecting Retirement Portfolios: Put and Call Options versus GLWBs." *Advisor Perspectives* (April 2013). https://www.advisorperspectives.com/articles/2013/04/30/the-best-solution-for-protecting-retirement-portfolios-put-and-call-options-versus-glwbs.

Chapter 3: Protect It

1. "Fact Sheet." Social Security Administration (February 2013).
2. "American Community Survey." US Bureau of the Census (2011).

3. "Disabled Worker Beneficiary Data." Social Security Administration (2012).
4. "Fact Sheet." Social Security Administration (December 2015).
5. "Genworth 2016 Cost of Care Survey." Genworth (April 2016). https://www.genworth.com/about-us/industry-expertise/cost-of-care.html.

Chapter 4: Take It

1. "Running Out of Money Is a Top Retirement Concern." AICPA (October 2016). http://www.aicpa.org/press/pressreleases/2016/pages/running-out-of-money-top-retirement-concern-financial-planners.aspx.
2. "Historical CD Interest Rate." ForecastChart. http://www.forecast-chart.com/rate-cd-interest.html.
3. "Economic News Release." Bureau of Labor Statistics (September 2016). http://www.bls.gov/news.release/cpi.nr0.htm.
4. William J. Wiatrowski, "The Last Private Industry Pension Plans: A Visual Essay." Bureau of Labor Statistics (December 2012). www.bls.gov/opub/mlr/2012/12/art1full.pdf.
5. Steven D. Levitt and Steven J. Dubner, "Why Should Suicide Bombers Buy Life Insurance?" in *SuperFreakonomics* (New York: HarperCollins Publishers, 2009).
6. Danielle Andrus. "Wade Pfau: Retirees Should Consider Reverse Mortgages." ThinkAdvisor (April 2016). http://www.thinkadvisor.com/2016/04/06/wade-pfau-retirees-should-consider-reverse-mortgage.

Chapter 5: Leave It

1. www.irs.gov.

Chapter 7: Choose It

1. Wade Pfau. "The Value of Financial Advice." McClean (July 2015). www.mcleanam.com/the-value-of-financial-advice.

2. Ibid.
3. Ibid.
4. "The Hidden Risk in Investment Portfolios." Goldman Sachs Asset Management (March 2017). https://www.gsam.com/content/gsam/us/en/individual/market-insights/gsam-connect/2017/the-hidden-risk-in-investment-portfolios.html.
5. Ron Sanders, "A Big Risk to Your Portfolio Is Hiding in Plain Sight." ONE Blog (March 2017). http://www.oneretirement.com/blog/a-big-risk-to-your-portfolio-is-hiding-in-plain-sight.
6. https://www.betterment.com/resources/research/tax-coordinated-portfolio-white-paper/.
7. Ibid.
8. www.cfp.net.
9. www.theamericancollege.edu.
10. www.fi360.com.

Made in the USA
Lexington, KY
14 September 2018